"I set goals, take control, drink out my own bottle. I make mistakes but learn from every one. And when it's said and done I bet this brother be a better one. If I upset you dont stress. Never forget, that God isn't finished with me yet."

- Tupac Shakur

SIDE A

The Black Collection (Intro)	13
Be The LP	15
My Rhyme Scheme	17
Call Me the Teacha (Hip Hop Culture and Authors Objectives)	19
Call and Response	21
Man in the Mirror	23
Dear Black Woman (Self Awareness and Self-Esteem)	25
Call and Response	27
Her Hijab	29
Earth to God	31
My Breath of Life (Cultural and Religious Practices)	33
Call and Response	35
Love for Badu	37
King	39
Appreciation Comes from the Roots	41
Closed Eye's and Relaxed (Pride and Appreciation for Black/African Culture)	43
Call and Response	45
The Price of History	47
Sounds of Freedom	49
When R.A.P Had Culture	51
Dab When You Know	53
Do You Know you're History? (Historical Impact and Present Day Disinterest)	57
Call and Response	59
Makings of the Greatest of All Time	61
What's Left?	63
We March for You	65
Queen Bree (Current Events and Social Injustice)	67
Call and Response	69
Birthmark Feelings	71
School Abuse	73
Mass Incarceration	75
Furlough Wand	78
Fatherly Request	80
The BP Party Today	81
Our Roots (Police Brutality and Survival Methods)	85
Call and Response	89
Naïve Revolution	91
Staring At Reality	93
Kick the Facts	95
The Scent of Reality	97
You Had Me	99
The A.I. Theory (Rebellious Mentality)	101
Call and Response	103

107	Newark What Happened?
109	Freestyle
111	Wu-Tang Clan is for the Kids
113	Hey Young World (Educating and Protecting the Youth)
115	Our Family Tree
117	Call & Response
119	Mornings with You
121	For the Moment
123	Worship You
125	Saturday with a Queen
127	Love Leaves The Room
129	Time 4 You
131	Walls
133	Forgive Me Janet (Relationships, Passion and Issues)
135	Call and Response
137	Video Sirens
139	Her Powers
141	A Jersey Thang
143	Cookout Weather
145	Weekend Visits
147	Thanksgiving Tips (Family and Friends)
149	Call and Response
151	Newark Bike Fest 2015
153	Beauty Becomes Ugliness
155	Digital People
157	Social Addiction (Social Media)
159	Call and Response
161	Dark Alliance
163	Paid In Full and Boring
165	Give More
167	Feeling Her (The Downfall Newark)
169	Focus and Learning While Burning
171	Origins Of Thuggery
173	Toe Tag Airs
175	Stop The Violence
177	Call and Response
179	How Are We?
181	Rise...(If You're Ready for Change)
183	Get In Formation
185	Be...for Newark (Rebuild)
187	Call and Response

SIDE B

The Metamorphosis of Black Culture

by: Baruti Libre Kafele

American society is heterogeneous, multi-cultural, and exists as the most fascinating and influential, populational organism of recent historical record. America contemporaneously is the most diverse country in the world that consists of cultural communities from across this 4.54-billion-year-old planet. There are 196 counties in the world and you can ultra-conservatively find at least one person from each country living in the United States of America. Hence, the United States' diversity of over 320 million people plays an unequivocal and undeniable role in the country's influence politically, sociologically, technologically, culturally, and militarily. America's unipolarity of power on the global sphere is accredited to its utilization of the genius and dexterity of groups of people globally. There is one group of people who did not immigrate to this country to seek the amenities, fruits, milk, or honey of Americanism but were instead dehumanized and commoditized as imports; they were African people or Black people. The irony is that Black people are the heartbeat of American society even though this may not be cognizable and realizable by the majority of the Black or African American population.

The concept of culture has a variety of definitions but for the contextual framework of this essay, I will use Dr. Neely Fuller's definition of culture from his book, The United Compensatory Code and System, as "the collective behavior of a group of people." Culture is inseparable to any aggregate of people and the most influential culture on the globe is African culture. African culture is very diverse but in the words of the multidisciplinary scholar Dr. Cheikh Anta Diop: "African people have a global cultural unity." From the Nubian, Kemetic (Egyptian), Ghanian, Malian, Songhai, Aksumite, Sabaen, Monomotoppan, and Mossian civilizations, Africa birthed influential empires that have impacted and introduced civilization to the world. Additionally, African people have introduced to the world, geometry, arithmetic, metallurgy, medicine, architecture (primarily pyramidal structures), philosophy, religiosity (which influenced Judaic-Christian thought), early forms of jurisprudence, political theory, astronomy, astrology, etc. Africa is 12 million square miles and the wealthiest piece of real estate on the globe due to its subsurface minerals which include gold, silver, platinum, diamonds, uranium, cobalt, chromium, titanium, oil, bauxite, and an abundance of others. Most importantly the most paramount resource from the continent of Africa which contributed to the development of American culture, is African or Black people who were imported to the Americas for the purpose of European and eventually Anglo-American prosperity.

African people were taken into captivity and transported to the Americas mainly via the trans-Atlantic Slave Trade that primarily consisted of molasses, rum and Africans. Africans first arrived in Colonial America in Jamestown, Virginia beginning in 1619 on the White Lion ship which was hi-jacked at sea by the Dutch from the Spaniards; 20 Africans were traded in exchange for food and supplies. African people were physically inflicted with indentured servitude that eventually became slavery from 1619 to the Union's victory in the Civil War in 1865, which was due to the 187,000 Africans who enlisted into the Union Army to defeat the Confederates. After emancipation, it was challenging for newly emancipated Black people to assimilate to American society and to become prosperous since we were deprived of education, literacy, and the basic human rights of life, liberty, property, the freedom of choice, the freedom of speech, the freedom of assembly, etc. Yet, through the proactivity and intelligence of our people, we managed to form institutions of vocational training, education, and engineering like the Tuskegee Institute and various other models throughout the war-torn South. Additionally, African Americans were elected as governors and Congressmen throughout the South. After the Civil War, we saw the augmentation of Black inventors, innovators, educators, and entrepreneurs who formed Black owned communities or "Black Wall Streets" in Richmond, Virginia; Rosewood, Florida; Tulsa, Oklahoma; Birmingham, Alabama; Tuskegee, Alabama; Durham, North Carolina, etc.

Even though African Americans were obtaining rights after the ratification of the 13th, 14th, and 15th Amendments of the U.S. Constitution, white Southerners - who were for the most part poor and lower middle class - were acrimonious and vindictive from their complacency in the Civil War and the upward mobility of Black people post the Union victory. This lead to the formation of white supremacist terrorist groups like the Ku Klux Klan (formed in Pulaski, Tennessee in 1866) who burned properties of Black people, killed, and continuously lynched Black people for the purpose of intimidation and to impede the progress of Black people in America. The concept of culture like any other organism is the adaptation and sometimes evolution of traits and behaviors of a group of people based on their situational circumstances. There were Black people who didn't allow the racism, vigilantism, and bigotry of white supremacy impede their progress, such as Black nationalists or nation builders. Booker T. Washington and Martin Delany formed their own vocational and industrial institutions and consulted Black entrepreneurs for the purpose of empowering our people. We also had inventors like George Washington Carter who discovered 300 ingredients from the peanut, Jan Matzeliger who immigrated to America via modern day Surname and invented the lasting shoe machine, Lewis Latimer who invented the carbon thread filament for the light bulb for Thomas Edison for the purpose of sustainable illumination, Elijah McCoy with his invention of the steam engine lubricator, and there was Madame C. J. Walker who became the first female self-made millionaire due to her cosmetologically products.

The intensity of blatant racism in the South after the enacting of Plessy v. Ferguson in 1896 and the Black Codes in order to repress the rights and liberties of Black people, we started to see the Great Migration from the South to the North to avoid the problems of the South; as people migrate, culture inevitably does the same. We were able to create genres of music like ragtime and jazz. We created our own dialect of English through the linguistic synthesis of English and West African languages and formed Gullah, which is spoken in South Carolina, and Louisianan Creole, which is spoken in Louisiana. Pushing through the struggles that were inflicted upon us, we migrated to the industrialized North and West to major cities: Philadelphia, Detroit, Chicago, Newark, Los Angeles, Las Vegas, Cleveland, Gary, Indiana, New York City, and various other metropolises in order to seek opportunities, jobs, and to have a safer life. By migrating to the industrialized and urbanized North, we started to create movements: the African Blood brothers, the Lost and Found Nation of Islam, the Moorish Science Temple, Marcus Mosiah Garvey's UNIA, and various other movements for the purpose of Black liberation and empowerment because we realized that the grass isn't always greener on the other side... and racism was as prevalent in the North as it was in the South.

Within the Black experience, there was a juxtaposition of Black Nationalist and Black Socialist movements generally in the urbanized North and integrationist movements inspired by Christianity in the South: the Southern Christian Leader Conference lead by Dr. Martin Luther King, the Congress for Racial Equality, and various other movements for egalitarianism and social justice for people of African descent. In the midst of these social movements, there were deliberate programs for the purpose of the infiltration, destabilization, discrediting, and dividing of these various movements and the vilification of our great leaders: Dr. Martin Luther King, Jr., Malcolm X, Stokely Carmichael (Kwame Ture), and Elijah Muhammad. This was done via the FBI Counter Intelligence Program in addition to governmental officials who were responsible for the influx of heroin and cocaine into African American communities in order to intoxicate and depoliticize our people. The purpose of these covert governmental programs was for the eventual proliferation and expansion of the prison industrial complex, which is a lucrative sector in the public and private sectors of American affairs, in order to alleviate the threat of Black people accumulating power by way of revolutionary means.

From the immense poverty and lack of opportunities through the power elite, mainly from the administrations of Nixon and Reagan, and the destabilization of influential movements like the Black Panther Party, we started to see the popularization of gang culture as an alternative to surviving and the accumulation of financial gratification. Additionally, we saw the changes in music from ragtime, to jazz, to the blues, to rhythm and blues, to soul, to funk, to a phenomena called hip hop which is a genre of music founded on August of 1973 at 1520 Sudwick Avenue in the Bronx, New York City. Hip hop became an artistic cultural expression and escapism from a lot of the societal ills inflicted upon our people. Hip hop is now a global and billion-dollar lifestyle brand and culture with multiple sub-genres and nine elements: b-boying, dj-aying, rapping, graffiti, knowledge, fashion, language, entrepreneurship, and beat boxing.

Enlightenment of factions of people within the African American experience surged the African and Black Consciousness Movements in different cultural communities. They were led by Afrocentric scholarly activists such as Dr. Yoseh Ben Jochanan, Dr. John

Henrick Clarke, Dr. Maulana Karenga, Dr. Jacob Carruthers, Dr. Molefi Asante, and various others.

Due to the various sociological phenomena in the Black community, Black culture is heterogeneous and the diffusion of cultural traits became more efficient due to globalization, technological advancement via the Internet, and the popularization of hip hop culture which is a subculture of Black culture. The advancement of Black culture is dependent upon the conscious and enlightened Black folks who are for the liberation and advancement of African people to become influential and sophisticated as it relates to the galvanization and organization of our people. Henceforth, institutions need to be created for the purpose of prosperity, power, and emancipating African people from mental oppression because the institution of slavery was, ironically, more mental than it was physical for people of African descent. In order to become a slave, one has to have cultural and historical amnesia. People of African descent today lack awareness of our glorious past and contributions to civilization due to the deculturalization of our people historically and contemporaneously, which was and still is the prerequisite for the lucrative economic system of slavery and the subservience of Black people in this European controlled and dominated world.

Black Thoughts

By: Keith Nweze

Perspective.
That's what I want to give.
 Free and full of cultural pride and information is how I want my Black people to live. My perspective on what motivates me and what motivates black people, while trying to bridge the gap between us and African people. I recently embraced my Nigerian heritage and it made me want to learn more. More about Nigeria, my land, my tribe, my family.

Free and full of cultural pride is how I want black folk to live.
Bridging the gap.

Connecting the experience and the culture, wanting the knowledge and experience from the Motherland and America to disperse into the black man, the black woman, the black child. Each poem in this collection discusses the subject or the obstacles in between these two entities. The separation, the miseducation, the distance between understanding and appreciation.

The Black Collection is a compilation of thoughts, emotions and experiences...personal experiences that are intertwined into specific themes. The open-ended questions that comprise the Call and Response section are incorporated to extend the conversation to your communities and circle of friends. It's the conversations of who we are and what we've been through as Black Americans and Africans who've migrated to America. A long overdue discussion that needs to take place between these splintered groups of people.

I arranged the language to pack information within a small amount of space, coupled with images to provide context to content, spark dialogue, and interactivity. Saying a lot with a little. That's the power of language, the power of images.

The foundation of The Black Collection series is built from the main modalities of my knowledge: Hip-Hop, TV/Movies, and books. In this particular volume, (Volume 1) it encompasses how Hip-Hop shaped my life. Additionally, I wanted to touch on how visual elements and social media currently impacts the issues prevalent in our community.

Our experiences shape us to become the person we will be in the future.

My drive to express myself using the written word was inspired by Tupac Shakur's The Rose That Grew from Concrete. This collection of poetry broke down the barrier of masculinity for me within this art form. As I digested the information and became immersed in his art, it no longer felt as if I had to be cliché with the "roses are red; violets are blue" type of flow. I realized that I could express my thoughts and feelings in ways that would resonate with those who read it, without conforming to a cookie-cutter template.

Tupac made it feel cool to be a poet.

Nasir (Nas) Jones mentally raised me. His ability to draw parallels impacted me greatly. His discography, specifically Illmatic and It Was Written, transformed me and incited the lyrical aspect of my life. The Black Collection pays homage to the Hip-Hop culture, as it is a part of who I am, a part of who we all are. The new wave of thought patterns that encouraged my writing abilities, specifically came from rap music.

So why Hip-Hop? Well, I believe a good Hip-Hop album should be diverse. There are two sides, side A and side B. While side A is for everyone, side B represents the "album cuts." These are personal and, in most cases, universally accepted. It's also subjective, which enriches the experience of the series. You'll notice this as you flow through each "track."

In side A, I discuss a broad range of topics, but specifically the means in which African American people embrace their culture and history, and how they interact with the police. I believe much of it has to do with our self-esteem and ancestral identification not being intact, how our pride and appreciation varies from strong and conscious, to passive and distant while trying to get a taste of the "American Pie." This disconnect proves that the further away you are from your true culture and religion, the more confusing you can be to yourself and society.

Those of the white culture are quite privy to and well versed on the ways in which they are viewed from the black perspective. In contrast, the knowledge of black culture, by black people, of their past and accomplishments, is not as strong as their counterparts. African American pride is controlled and suppressed by this continuous cycle of misinformation and miseducation.

It's important to recognize the historical impact of African Americans in this country and understand why there is fear towards us from those of the white culture. Intellect, as they see it, is dangerous and the more they can decentralize the intellect of the black man, the easier it is to maintain control. In this series, I wanted to encourage black people to educate themselves on not only their history, but also the history of this country and its systems. It is through education that black people can be and remain liberated.

In side B, I capture the appreciation and subtleties of life and nature, my love for Newark, New Jersey, and Essex County, along with the positive and negative outlooks on community affairs. There are so many people who want to do something, but don't want to give up what they have to make an impact. We're all, in some ways, chasing money. That chase either affects or is affected by our current events. There's a paradigm shift happening that makes me beg the question: is it possible to rebuild our communities? Is it physically, emotionally, and economically possible to rebuild our communities?

The strength of black culture is more than just its music, it's the family unit. There are many taboos and clichés that are dominate within the black family unit. I wanted to capture the relationship with father and daughter, which is often dismissed or overshadowed, as well as capture the conflict of a mother's sacrifice to do something positive and the grandmother who steps in to fill that void.

The Black Collection is designed to exude positivity, to mend relationships, to encourage others to make love and be passionate, to trigger a deeper interest in one another. I made sure to include a writing space in the back of the book for you to jot down your thoughts or send me questions. And yes, I will answer them. Don't be shy.

I want to be an agent of change – what many call a thought leader. For me it's not just about compiling a bunch of words in a book and selling it to you. It's more than that. It's about reigniting the fire in all of us to bring unity back into our collective culture and community. It is my belief that BLACK is nothing more than a political identity and that we're all Africans who happen to live in America.

13

THE BLACK COLLECTION VOL. 1 : KEITH NWEZE

INTRO

In America,
there's 40 million ways to be black.
If you listen close
to the rhythmic landscape
you'll hear the thoughts,
emotions and experiences
of black culture
inside our raps.
This book
is the black film
inside the grey cassette tape.
My black face
comes from the same place
as your black face.
These black lyrics
were designed to defy the gravity of race.
These songs
were produced by a dignified,
yet classified
black man that has something to say…

Press play.

THE BLACK COLLECTION VOL. 1 : KEITH NWEZE

BE THE LP

You be the needle.
I'll be the LP.

Let's
make songs
for the people's eyes.
Songs
for the old and young,
Songs
that sting like a battle cry.

Let's
embody the rhythm and pain
spinning inside our
brains
like trains
traveling through gritty city life.

You be the needle.
I'll be the LP.

Let's
embody a young KRS-One
dressed in green,
or the black Raiders hat
NWA wore when they hit the scene.
Label me rebellious
like Chuck D and Public Enemy.
My messages
are direct teachings
from Eric B. and Rakim.
Nas and Wu-Tang
embodying 5% wisdom,
mixed with Ghetto Boy's
and A Tribe Called Quest's vision.
Vocals of Biggie and Pac
peacefully blending.
Can you hear me?

You be the needle.
I'LL BE THE LP.

My rhymes
are truth to morning,
bringing light to time.
At night my child-like imagination
writes life into these lines.

You pick.

Doesn't matter
if it's transitions by B.I.G.
or Jay-Z's compounding
you're gonna feel
my rhyme scheme.

You pick.

Doesn't matter
if it's AZ's metaphors
or Nas' similes
you're gonna feel
my rhyme scheme.

You pick.

Doesn't matter
if it's Tupac's internals
or Kendrick's couplets
you're gonna feel
my rhyme scheme.

You pick.

Doesn't matter
if it's Big Daddy Kane's
rapid flow
or Kool G Rap's sonnets
you're gonna feel
my rhyme
scheme.

God generates.
Man creates.

Call me the Teacha.
A message poet,
far from a preacher.

Call me the Temple of Hip Hop.
The speaker that made the
Stop the Violence Movement hot.

Call me a humanist.
Fully aware of the Greeks bearing gifts.

Call me righteous.
 Making it known
the Police ain't shit.

Call me criminal minded.
"Sound of da Police"
remains timeless.

Call me the truth
with more life to give.

Rap is something you do,
Hip Hop is something you live.

God generates.
Man creates.

- Can rap music be used to promote political and social awareness?

- If you can record a song, what message or content would you use in the song?

- What do you think of the words nigger and nigga?

- Do you think African Americans have ways of imposing limits on black identity?

MAN IN THE MIRROR

Mr. Man in the mirror,
your
natural features
are worthy
and unique.

Mr. Man in the mirror,
your mask
won't cure
or hide
your shattered
self-esteem.

Pride
broken down
like oxen.

Fractured from carrying
centuries
of lies within.

Self-love
is not so vile a sin.

But self-neglect
is blatant
disrespect.

THE BLACK COLLECTION VOL. 1 : KEITH NWEZE

DEAR BLACK WOMEN

Divine beauty,
don't change a thing.

Does the make-up
of your complexion,
define
true
visual faith?

Dear Black Queens,
trust and believe
God don't make mistakes.

In our darkest dreams,
your beauty illuminates.

Don't change a thing.

Be proud
of who you are.

Scream

in contempt
if society tries
to feed you lies
and ultimatums,
persuading you away
from your exquisitely
crafted truth.

Don't change a thing.

No matter the money
or temptations soaring
from the stars.

Don't change a thing.

Decide which
thoughts you voice
and the actions you take,
or they will define you.

Don't change a thing.

You're perfectly beautiful the way you are.

- What does being "Black" mean to you?
- Are there particular and/or necessary characteristics of blackness?
- Who defines black culture and beauty and are they credible sources?
- What are the factors that prompt African Americans to get cosmetic surgery?

THE BLACK COLLECTION VOL. 1 : KEITH NWEZE

CALL & RESPONSE

SELF-AWARENESS & SELF-ESTEEM

HER HIJAB

Exploring inner peace,
exchanging philosophies
with a beautified Queen.
The fabric
modestly
gracing her skin
shows the texture
of her deen.
Her treasures,
held inside
like a pearl
within its shell.
Her hijab
represents
the dignity
she has for self.
Some say
it's too conventional.
Others say
the opposite
is too liberal.
Yet,
no opinions
can grasp
Allah's vision.
And in this vision
his clothes
are above
comprehension.

THE BLACK COLLECTION VOL. 1 : KEITH NWEZE

EARTH TO GOD

Earth
whispers love
to God.

"You possess more
knowledge,
wisdom,
and understanding
than the galaxy possesses stars.
You
are a King,
a Supreme Being in the flesh.
You are a mathematician
a scientist,
the arm
leg
leg
arm
head
willing to take
and pass life's
spiritually
and culturally biased test.
Your radiance
is a pillar of fire at night
often clouded by day.
Your light
is the guidance
youth
will need
to find their way…"

In response,
with culture,
power,
equality, and love in arms,
God
gives Earth
the moon and stars.

37

MY BREATH OF LIFE

Engulfed by your aura
like weed and P-Funk.
Listening to Mama's Gun.
Harmonizing life's heighten chorus
while caressing each other's ankhs.

Since we
left the womb
we've been looking
for the same comfort.
A unifying sign
to nurture our self-worth.

No need to search
for God's tears,
or fear joy
leaving a King's eyes.
My reign needs your vibes.
My spiritual insight,
my Nile,
my breath of life...

- How powerful is knowledge of self?
- What in your opinion should be the aim of education?
- What position does religion play in the modern Black community?
- Is Muslim culture and practices fully understood by American society?

THE BLACK COLLECTION VOL. 1 : KEITH NWEZE

CALL & RESPONSE
CULTURAL AND RELIGIOUS PRACTICES

40

LOVE FOR BADU

Your lips
stimulate my heartbeat.
Your poetry travels through me.
On and on we go.

Kindred spirits
wrapped inside the essence
of Neo-Soul.
On and on we go.

Spinning through
your
pro-black songs.
Your Love songs.
Your sociopolitical songs.
Your spiritual songs.
Your telephone songs.

Hearing your flow,
feeling your seductive eyes,
right down to the beauty mark
on your nose.

I'm alive
right there with you,
On and on we go.

THE BLACK COLLECTION VOL. 1 : KEITH NWEZE

KING

43

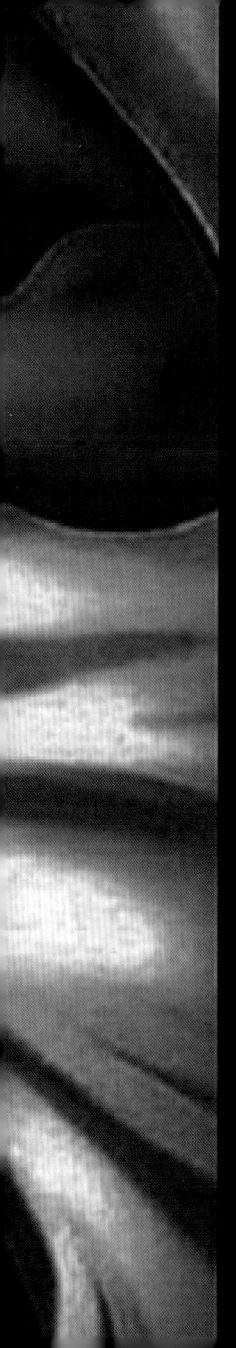

I no longer wait
for a King,
my raging heart
now only waits for him.

He's my Zulu.
My warrior spirit,
my conquering Hannibal.

He treats me
like Queen Sheba,
like the Goddess of Africa,
like nature's purest emblem.

Describing and taking
my beauty from ancient Venus
to the mythical Helen.

Clothed in the smoothest silk
and finest linen.

For him,
I patiently wait
in heat
with my soul at ease,
undressed.

Sweet king
of life's
evergreen land,
my placid blue sea.

His love
is dessert to me.

APPRECIATION COMES FROM MY ROOTS

Got a deep appreciation
for the natural.
It's in my roots.

With 2 hands,
I feel you,
I dig you.
Got a soft spot
for the orobo.
Blame it on the
Ibo blood
pumping inside me.
That Naija ancestry.
Good jollof.
Obsessed
with the fem petite.

Thick flesh,
sturdy
and sweet.

I love
every inch,
every size,
every root from you.

THE BLACK COLLECTION VOL. 1 - KEITH NWEZE

CLOSED EYES, RELAXED

Closed eyes,
relaxed.

Embracing the vibes,
the fact
that your Black
and you're the shit.

You embody,
a 90's era
revivalist.

A fluid mix
of Lauryn Hill
and Rah Digga
spitting that shit.

Your body
and brain
display
an evenly shaped
instrumentalist.

Your
insane afro
smoothly flows
towards brilliance.

You're militant,
unafraid to debate politics.
Staring
those racist Capitalist
in the face;
willing to reorganize
our economic interest.

But today
you lay in the shade,
eyes closed,
completely relaxed.
Baskin'
in the fact
that you're the shit
and you're
Black.

- 📼 Do you think some Black people need to be more open-minded about what it means to be Black?

- 📼 Where does self-esteem and pride come from?

- 📼 Would relationships in the Black community be stronger if we were more culturally aware?

- 📼 Does being Black mean something different now than it meant three or four decades ago?

CALL & RESPONSE

PRIDE AND APPRECIATION FOR BLACK/AFRICAN CULTURE

THE PRICE OF HISTORY

Can't deny
the beauty of history.
The Motherland's wealth
and resources are no mystery.

Societies built off her
sweat and gold.
The texture of Kenté cloth
has always been in the fold.

Yet we only feel paper,
refusing to mix
new concepts with old.
Selling everything,
including our culture and souls.

Writing on the phone
in front of a typewriter
asking myself,
"can one respect their origin
and grow on a popstar's bankroll?"

Eddie Griffin once told us
it's rare a pro-black entertainer
makes it out of Hollywood whole.

THE BLACK COLLECTION VOL. 1 : KEITH NWEZE

SOUNDS OF FREEDOM

If you listen
you can hear
Africa's underbelly
pounding beneath.

Scratched,
sequenced
and mixed in the streets.
The sound of freedom
bounces off the concrete.

Heritage and history
over a foreign baseline
described by the Djembe.

Stories and vibes of Griots.

The ability to hear and feel
lies inside the melody;
the movement touches the eyes
and ears of harmony.

Get your hands up
if your down to be free.

Get your hands up
if your down to be free.

THE BLACK COLLECTION VOL. 1 : KEITH NWEZE

WHEN RAP HAD CULTURE

When Rap had culture.
And African medallions graced
every neck and shoulder.
And the unity pressed on Malcolm X t-shirts
hit the establishment like a raging boulder.
And the lyrics were an assault
against the New World Order.
And the Righteous Paroled Poets
begin to followed Allah's way.
And the language the kid's rapped
were direct teachings Clarence 13X conveyed.
Happy supreme degree day
to all the God's,
Earth's
and Young Soldier's.

When Rap had culture.
Before the corporate takeover.
Before the restructured deals
and commercial radio payola.
Before keeping it real
raised the death quota.
We acknowledged and treated our Art
and Culture like the backbone
to our society.
We allowed ourselves
to be a masterpiece
and a work in progress,
simultaneously.

When Rap had culture.

THE BLACK COLLECTION VOL. 1 : KEITH NWEZE

DAB WHEN YOU KNOW

Dab
when you know
color is not the issue,
class is...

Dab
when the boycotts are through
and Beyonce's money
is still supporting
Black activists... wait...

Dab
when they acknowledge the truth,
the media is funded
by racists...

Dab
for the Cam Newton inside you,
for the obstacles you hurdled
to be your best...

Dab
when you know
America values our history,
our Pharaohs
old or new...

Dab
when you find
comfort and survival,
the source of heritage
beaming inside
you...

DO YOU KNOW YOU'RE HISTORY?

Do you know the people
in and around our history?
Do you understand the affects
those people have on our mentality?
Do you love them more
than you love me?

Does their fair skin make you
forget what happened in Haiti?
Do you know who
blew the nose off the Sphinx?

Will you wave anyone of the 54 African flags
for the thousands
murdered in Kenya
and Nigeria last week?
Will you protest and change your profile
pics for causes that aren't trendy?

Do you understand
that there are no oppressed people
more committed
to the oppressor's culture and history
than we?

THE BLACK COLLECTION VOL. 1 : KEITH NWEZE

RAPPING WITH THE PRESIDENT

A booming presence said
"Those Republican supporters
need to support more
than Trump and war!!"
It's hard to ignore
the destructive sound bouncing hard
off the floor
in a room
designed in the finest decor.
1 daughter
in the background
overhearing 2 distinct voices rap
'The World is Yours'.
Caught between
greater and lesser power's.
Conversing about the urban economic
condition during the God hour.
Searching inward for the right time
and place
to do more...

THE BLACK COLLECTION VOL. 1 : KEITH NWEZE

- 📼 Is African (American) culture and history beautiful to you?

- 📼 What influence does Hip Hop have on American Culture?

- 📼 What effects does the American educational system have on historical pride in the Black community?

- 📼 How do we create more Barack Obamas?

THE BLACK COLLECTION VOL. 1 : KEITH NWEZE

CALL & RESPONSE

HISTORICAL IMPACT AND PRESENT DAY DISINTEREST

MAKINGS OF THE GREATEST OF ALL TIME

Talking about
defining moves in one's prime.
Waiting for a fresh line –
debating character
and
what constitutes true talent
inside one's mind.
From Trayvon Martin hoodies
to "I Can't Breathe" black tees.

From delivering stop the gun violence PSA's
to awarding scholarships
to ghetto kids
who perform scholastically.

Some argue their points intelligently
while others yell passionately
about championship performances,
ignoring racial issues
and societal crimes.

Objectivity
completely missing
getting the bread lined,
debating the greatest of all time.

THE BLACK COLLECTION VOL. 1 : KEITH NWEZE

WHAT'S LEFT?

After the war
with the Southern confederation,
emancipation,
reconstruction,
World War II's need for mass production,
and
the outsourcing of industrialization…

What's left?

After the bus boycotts
and voter registration,
segregation,
nationalism,
heroin contamination,
employment evacuation
and gentrification…

What's left?

After revised racism
and low expectations,
commercialization,
socialization,
classifications
and poor education…

What's left?

THE BLACK COLLECTION VOL. 1 : KEITH NWEZE

WE MARCH FOR YOU

Because you
fed them
to make us
strong enough
to stand on 2 feet.

Over 1 million
of your babies
march in unity
on the land
where the American eagle eats.

Following the minister's lead
are the Kings
raised by resilient Queens
thoroughly trained by the FOI
during MGT and GCC.

Marching with conscious pride,
like Public Enemy,
knowing and understanding
the sacrifices made
for our lives.

Motivated by you,
feeling your
tears fall
from the sky.

THE BLACK COLLECTION VOL. 1 : KEITH NWEZE

We march on D.C.
for you,
because you fed
baby Capitalism
as she sucks Mother Africa dry!

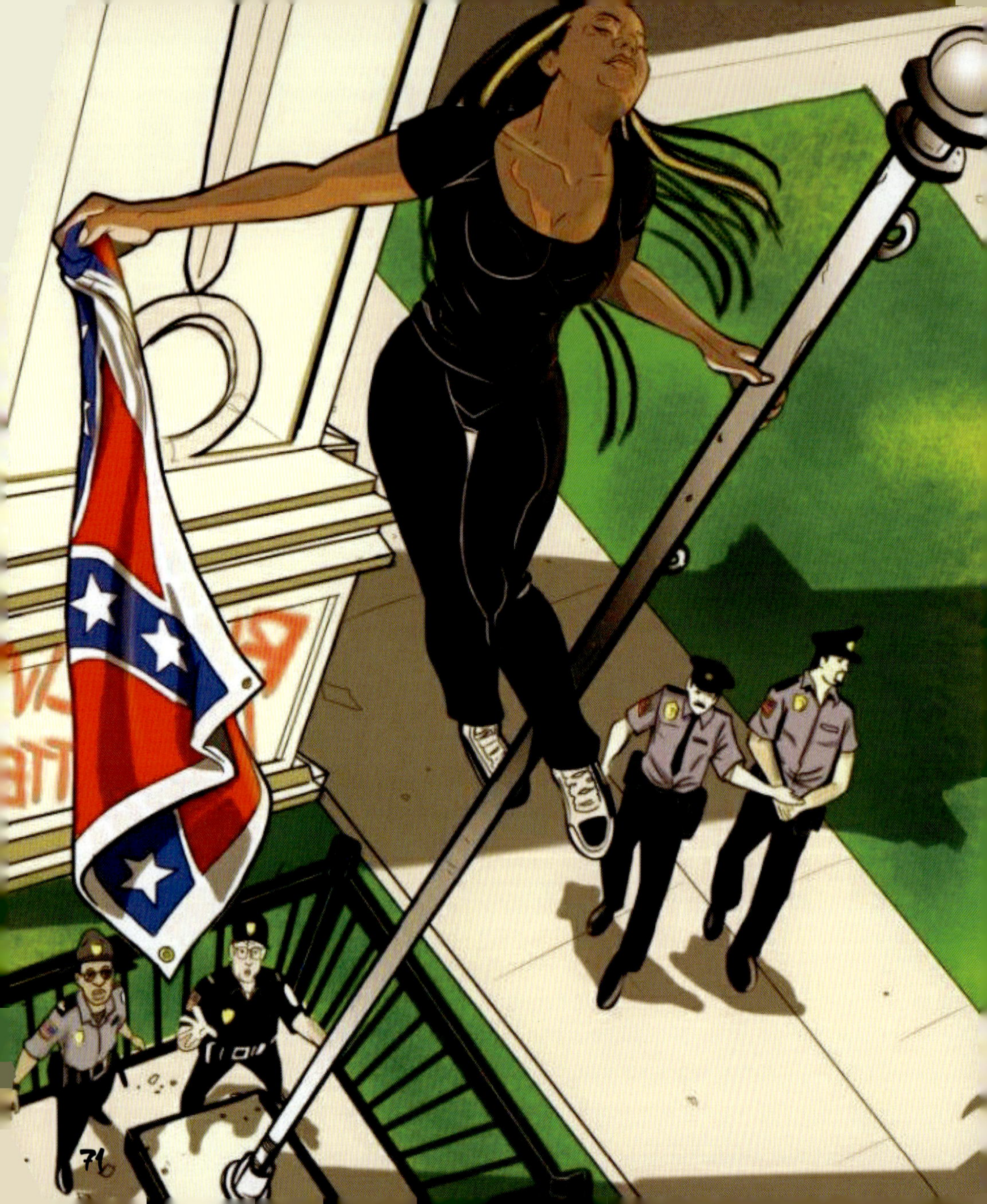

THE BLACK COLLECTION VOL. 1 : KEITH NWEZE

QUEEN BREE

Black Lives Matter!
Black Lives Matter!
Black Lives Matter!
Black Lives Matter!

Dressed
in all black,
Queen Bree
couldn't of have been any badder
as she defiantly screamed,
"I Did it
because
I am free!"

Freedom rings -
clutching their flag,
love swings
from Queen Bree's
dreads,
flowing unity.

Eyes closed
embodying peace,
watching brutality
with a growing hate.
9 innocent lives
murdered senselessly,
as her beauty
tries to keep her feelings
from registering on her face.
Knowing the fate
that awaits her
in such a dangerously
racist place.

▣ What are the next impending obstacles facing Black people?

▣ Why is it important to protest and march?

▣ Does the African American community embrace cultural issues more than societal issues? Do we know the difference between the two?

▣ In your opinion, does social or political change stem from economic or psychological causes?

THE BLACK COLLECTION VOL. 1 : KEITH NWEZE

CALL & RESPONSE

CURRENT EVENTS AND SOCIAL INJUSTICE

74

BIRTHMARK FEELINGS

Indiscrimination is a bitch...
Doc, I'm feeling
the hardships of society's
ignorance...
I'm feeling
the awkwardness of decades,
the weight of centuries
shackled to our legs.
I'm feeling dizzy
trying to find a breath
that will accept the concept
of my people living free...
Doc!
while I search for this reality,
can you remove this giant
birthmark from me?

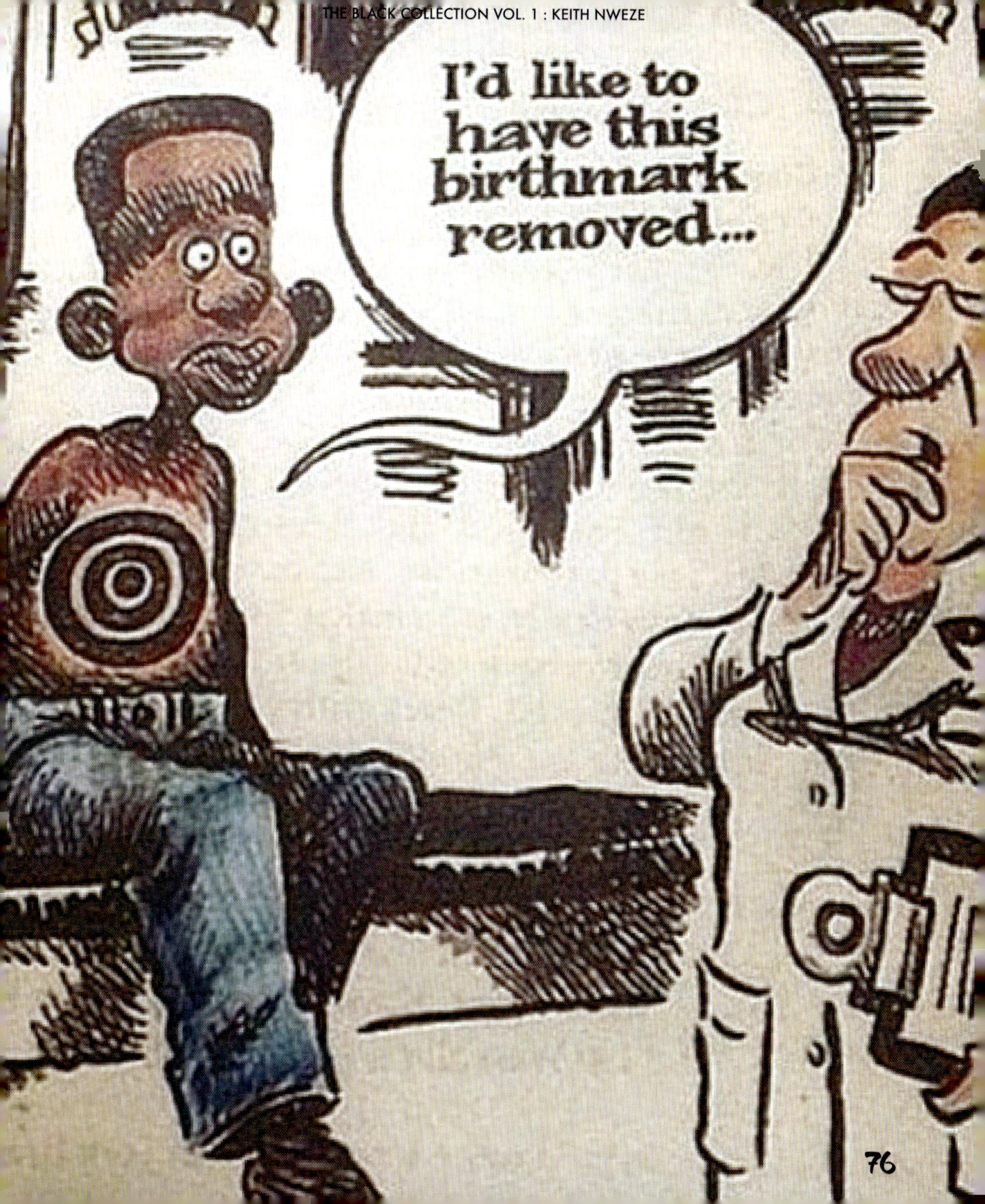
I'd like to have this birthmark removed...

SCHOOL ABUSE

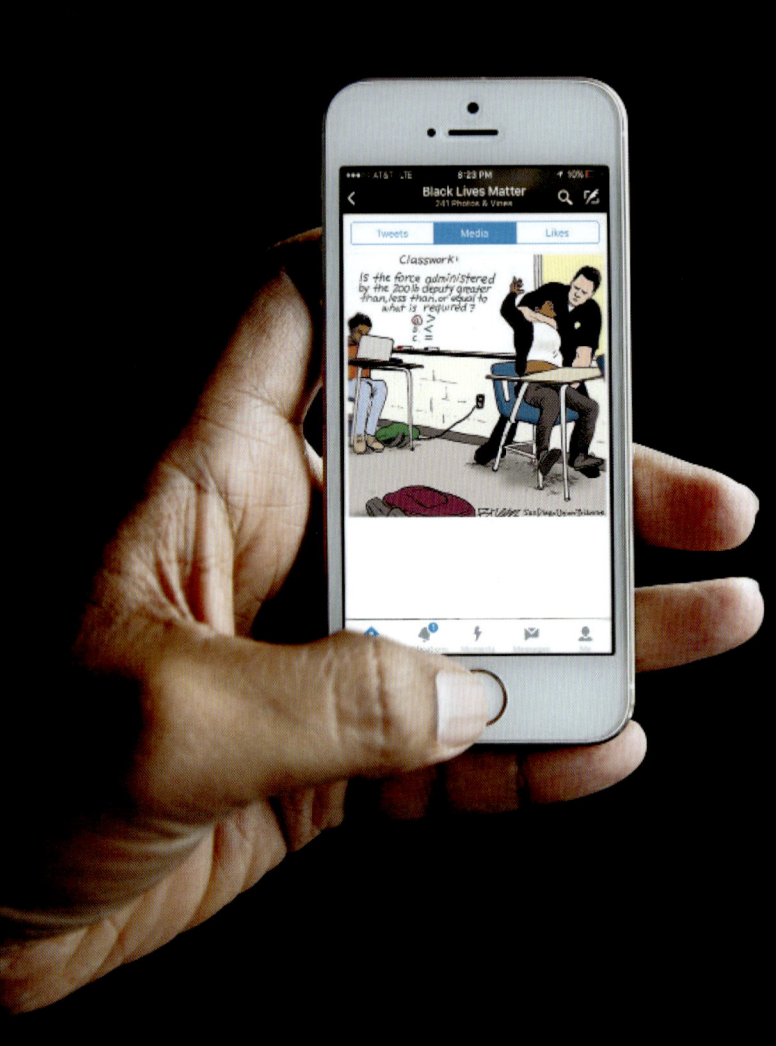

Parents just don't understand.

Kids,
here's the answers
for life's pop quiz
only if you're interested
in the truth, that is?

We know the institutions
that educate you
are isolated
and protected
from review.

Never see yourself
as the world
perceives you.

Never allow yourself
to be marginalized
by society's
inferior view.

Never let
ignorance
touch
or define you.

Kids,
the force
administered
by the 200lb deputy
is unequal treatment
you should
never
get used to.

We know
the corresponding folk
don't speak for you.

Never submit
or obey
the authority
of their broken rules.

MASS INCARCERATION

Mass incarceration.

Public Defenders
meet and plea.
The criminal cases
heard in the urban courts
end up laborers
in the penitentiary.

Mass incarceration.

To be free,
to imagine
yourself truly free
but held captive
in profit prisons
between the tight
bureaucratic grips
of a capitalistic society.

Mass incarceration.

THE BLACK COLLECTION VOL. 1 : KEITH NWEZE

JARROD BROWN

ID NO. 112192
MAY 2 15

CHARGE: CRIMINAL JUSTICE

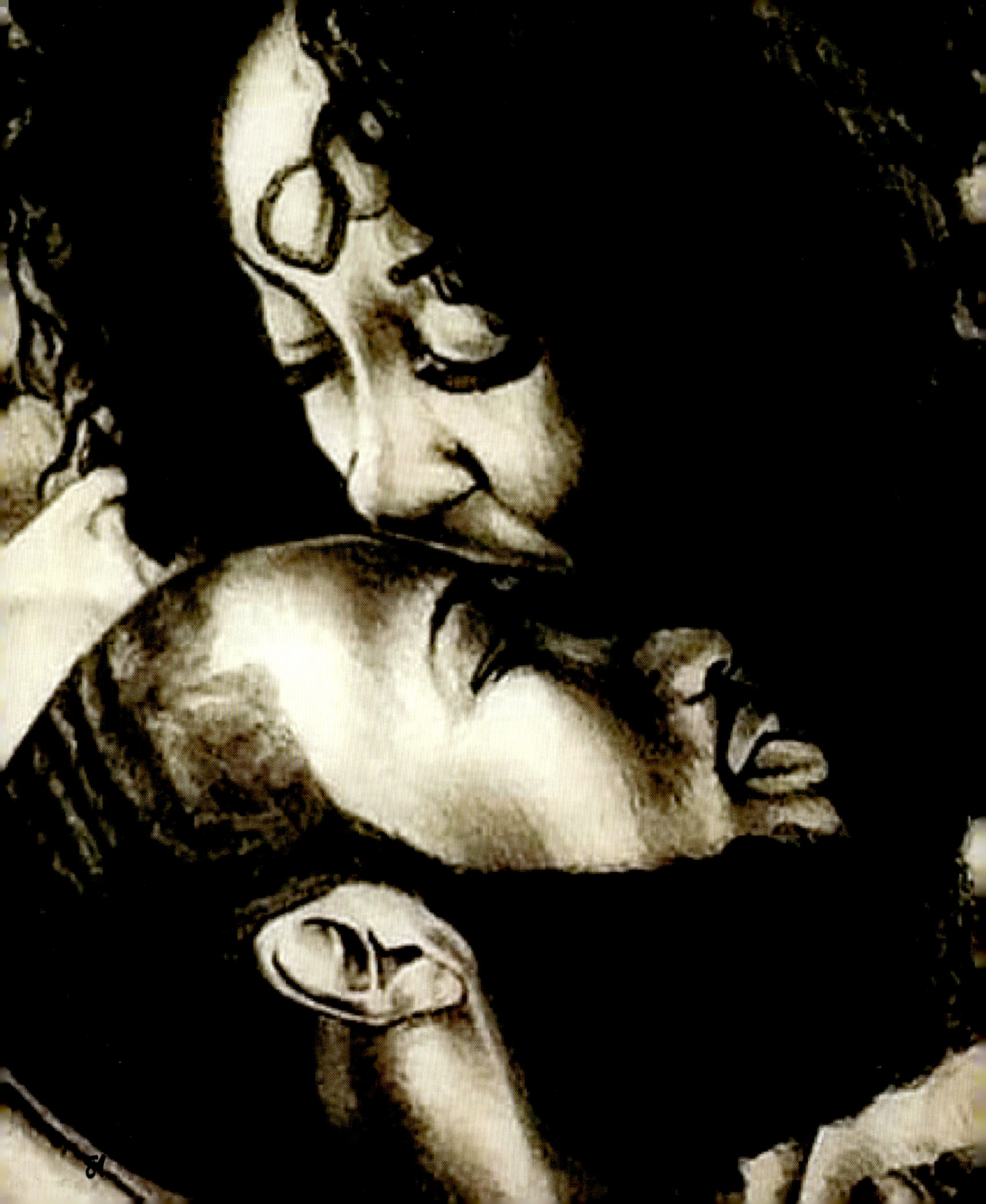

FURLOUGH WAND

She kissed me on the forehead
when I said I miss him.
Her comfort twirling,
twisting
'round the wilderness on my chin.
Living with regret,
drowning in my own sin.
A deep reality
welled up
from within.

Suffocated by hope.
Deflated by hope.

Harvesting time
lost in an election year.
Calculating the cost,
the league of legal lies
litigating my fears.

Wish Obama would wave his furlough wand
and make my brother reappear.
Wish he didn't have to be patient
and strong
while he sits in a prison camp
full of guilty volunteers.

FATHERLY REQUEST

83

Collect call accepted.
Hearing evolution
inside the inner workings of stress.
More like Malcolm now than Detroit red,
so I accepted his fatherly request.

Considered myself
blessed
even in the small role
I'm asked to play.

A disciple of love,
delivering a gift,
an encrypted message
to his daughter
on her birthday.

The voice over the phone,
doing time
for survival crimes
committed yesterday.
Mentally strong,
emotionally alone,
far away.
It's been years
since he's kissed his baby
on her born day.

It's been years
since she saw
her father's face.

It's been years
since she last saw me,
with a smile and soft eyes.

Kneeling to deliver his message
and their favorite snack together,
2 small sweet potato pies.

Letting time fill our stomachs,
we ate memories in peace.

Feeling the reality in my gut,
my Queen,
why does the pain
run so deep?

THE BP PARTY TODAY

The memory and impact of Huey,
Bobby,
Bunchy,
Fred,
Emory,
and Stokely
scares the establishment.

Those young,
naïve,
brave kids
with common sense.

Passionately reciting
political poetry,
dancing to upbeat
love songs.

Doing the Philly Dog,
selling fish dinners,
weed,
and Chairman Mao's
Red Book
at house parties
to liberate
the weak
and the strong

This is how the youth
thought back then.

Profits going to the
Ten-Point Program
to fund what they
truly believed in.

Employment,
decent housing,
true education,
the immediate end to
police brutality
and the power
to determine
the destiny
of their community,
ultimately becoming
public enemy #1,
jailed
or murdered
in an attempt to be free.

Birthing
the single household generation,
the 'running man'
became the popular
survival dance
one now executes
for peace.

A celebratory demand given
by the mother's and women
who witnessed the afterlife
parties thrown routinely
in the late 60s and 70s.

Running from the movement,
right into crack cocaine in the 80s,
chasing money in the early 90s.

Mom and Dad showed their
kids
the Kid 'n' Play dance
after working 7 days a week
on swollen legs and feet.

Joy made them
want to live,
surely as pain
taught them how to live.

The heart
of the Black Power movement
was once ran by kids
with brains full of ambition
stuck in the tsunami of politics.

Sitting in jail
or in a pool of blood,
leaving fatherless seeds.

Staring at the ground,
thinking about yesterday
watching the silly dances
done
by a new generation
the establishment
happily, labels:
"Bastards of the Party.

87

THE BLACK COLLECTION VOL. 1 : KEITH NWEZE

OUR ROOTS

Our roots have been through it.

Pulled
so far away
from the movement
that we no longer possess
the desire to resist.

Gone
from our current mental fire
is the strength to hold
and use
that once proud
Black Fist.

So here's the nappy,
painfully rough truth
for every actual
and perceived Negro.
A small, select group
inside the boys in blue
represent
the institutional control
that combs the catacombs
of the ghetto.

Trying to weed our roots from our home.

THE BLACK COLLECTION VOL. 1 : KEITH NWEZE

IF WE'RE DYING

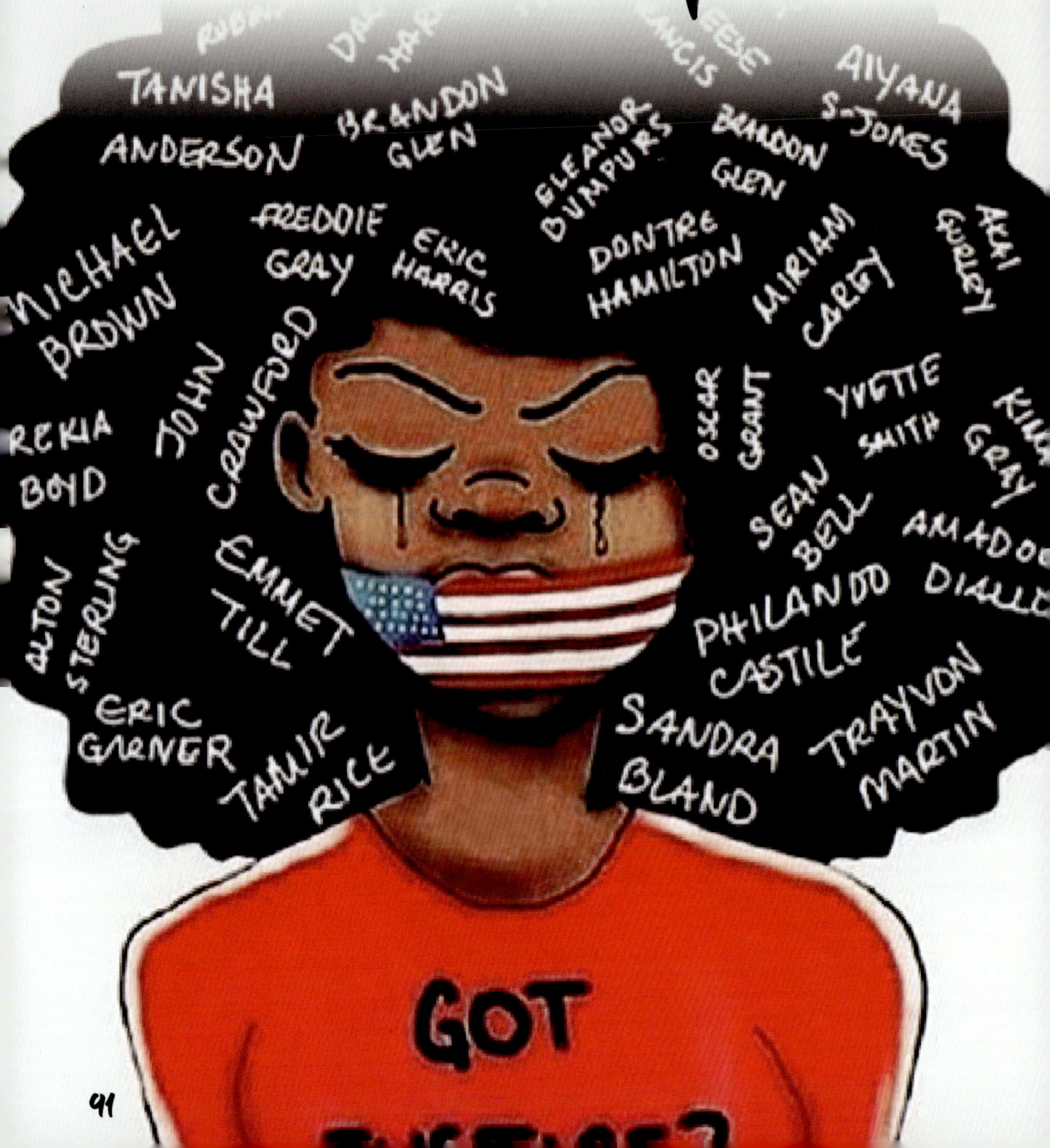

If we're dying,
I'm dying.
Watching the ongoing results
of police brutality.
Black lives that matter
splattered all over TV.
Who's responsible for the climate
of this country?
Seems like space
and the sky get more respect
than the bloody bodies laying
in the wet soil of disbelief.

If we're dying,
I'm dying.
You'll hear the cries
of Africa's underbelly
pounding beneath.
Where's all my powerful voices,
where's Jay-Z?
Searching for the black elite,
all the righteous
brothers and sisters
willing to teach.

If we're dying,
I'm dying.
But America know this,
our community will raise
strong
and intelligent black babies,
before your lead hits our head.

- 📼 Are Black people born with a target on their backs?
- 📼 Does the school administration need retraining to cater to black students?
- 📼 How many convictions are by-products of Meet and Plea circumstances?
- 📼 Who profits off mass incarceration?
- 📼 What effect does prison have on children and family members?

THE BLACK COLLECTION VOL. 1 : KEITH NWEZE

CALL & RESPONSE

POLICE BRUTALITY AND SURVIVAL METHODS

NAIVE REVOLUTION

Naïve revolution,
please find and align
all the lost and confined
minds.

The one's
on the
Footlocker lines.
Summer Jam tickets lines.
Liquor store lines.
Cocaine lines.
Prescription pill lines.
Abortion clinic lines.
Welfare lines.
Unemployment lines.
Picket lines.
Lives are on the line.

Dying,
or sentenced

25 to Life
for survival crimes.
Drug- related crimes.
Black on Black crimes.
Cultural crimes.
Self-esteem crimes.
Conspiracy to expose their
crimes.

Naïve revolution,
please give solutions
to the house nigger's
thoughts
and bolt cutters
to the field nigger's brain.

As long as
we're all on the
same page,
we have nothing to lose

But Our Chains!

THE BLACK COLLECTION VOL. 1 : KEITH NWEZE

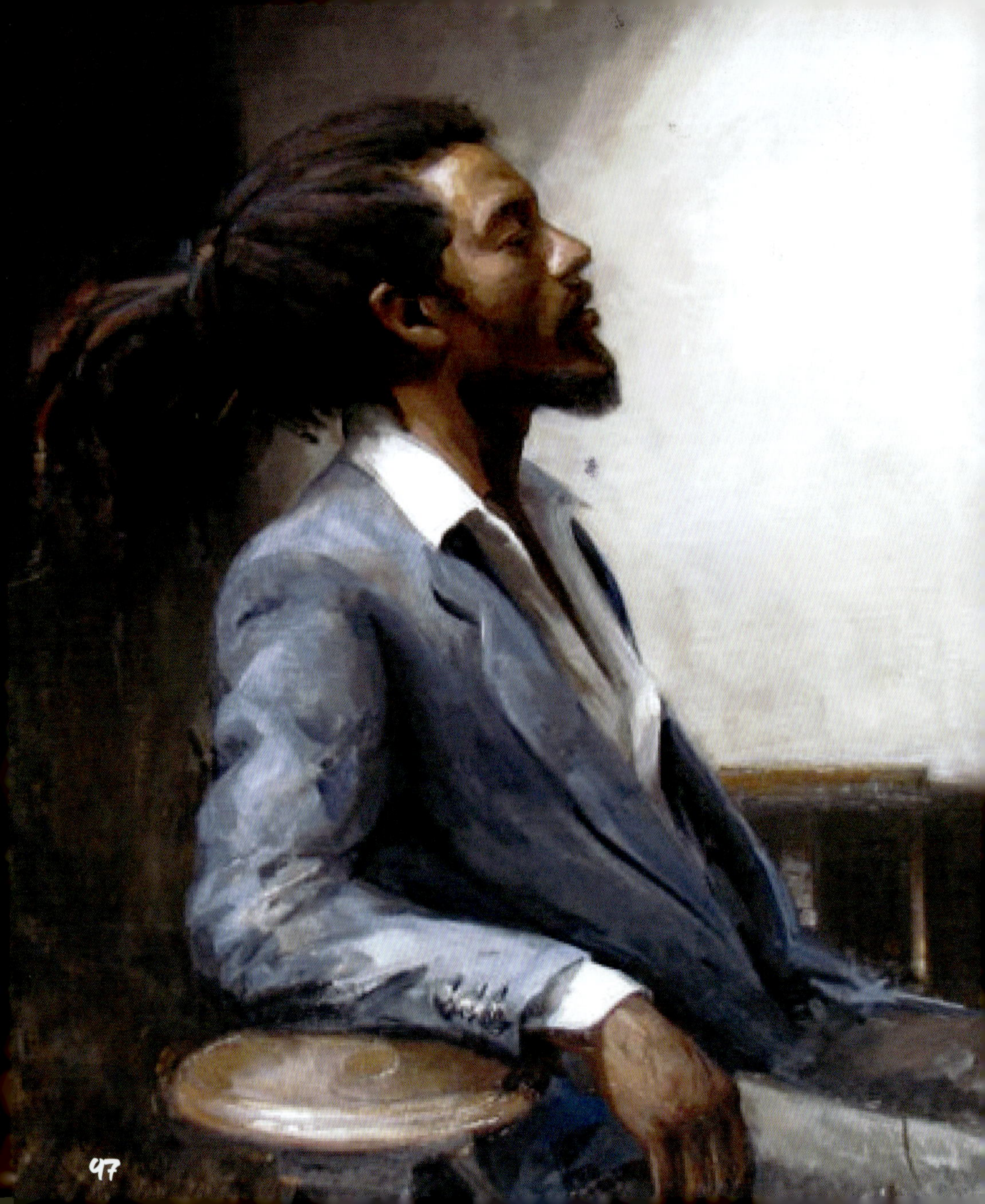

STARING AT THE WORLD

Can one
pimp a butterfly
and maintain the sanity
of its original features?

Young girls and mass murderers
are tender hearted creatures.

Last night I shed tears
but did not cry
for the homicides committed
in Orlando over gay rights.

Last night I shed tears
but did not cry
for the mass shootings
in Opelousas, Louisiana
over civil rights.

I grieved in silent outrage.
Clinching my teeth,
in silent outrage.

I stared at the world,
triggers pointed at my face,
while I searched for a freedom
that would last.

I stared at the world,
triggers pointed at my face,
wondering if the President
was the hope for the future
or the guilt of the past?

KICK THE FACTS

Ax kick
all the bullshit stereotypes.
Spin kick
all the hood perceptions
and Reality TV hype.
Fly kick
all the hypocrites
and oppressors down
to destroy black lives.
Push kick
all the media boundaries
while rapping
Kendrick Lamar's "Alright."
Roundhouse kick
all the domestics
abusing their wives.
Back kick
all the child support
and warrants locking down
our lives.
Side kick
all the processed foaod
given to get by.
Fire kick
the educational
and political
system that taught us lies.
Just know
and understand
the target
before you pick the fight.

THE BLACK COLLECTION VOL. 1 : KEITH NWEZE

THE SCENT OF REALITY

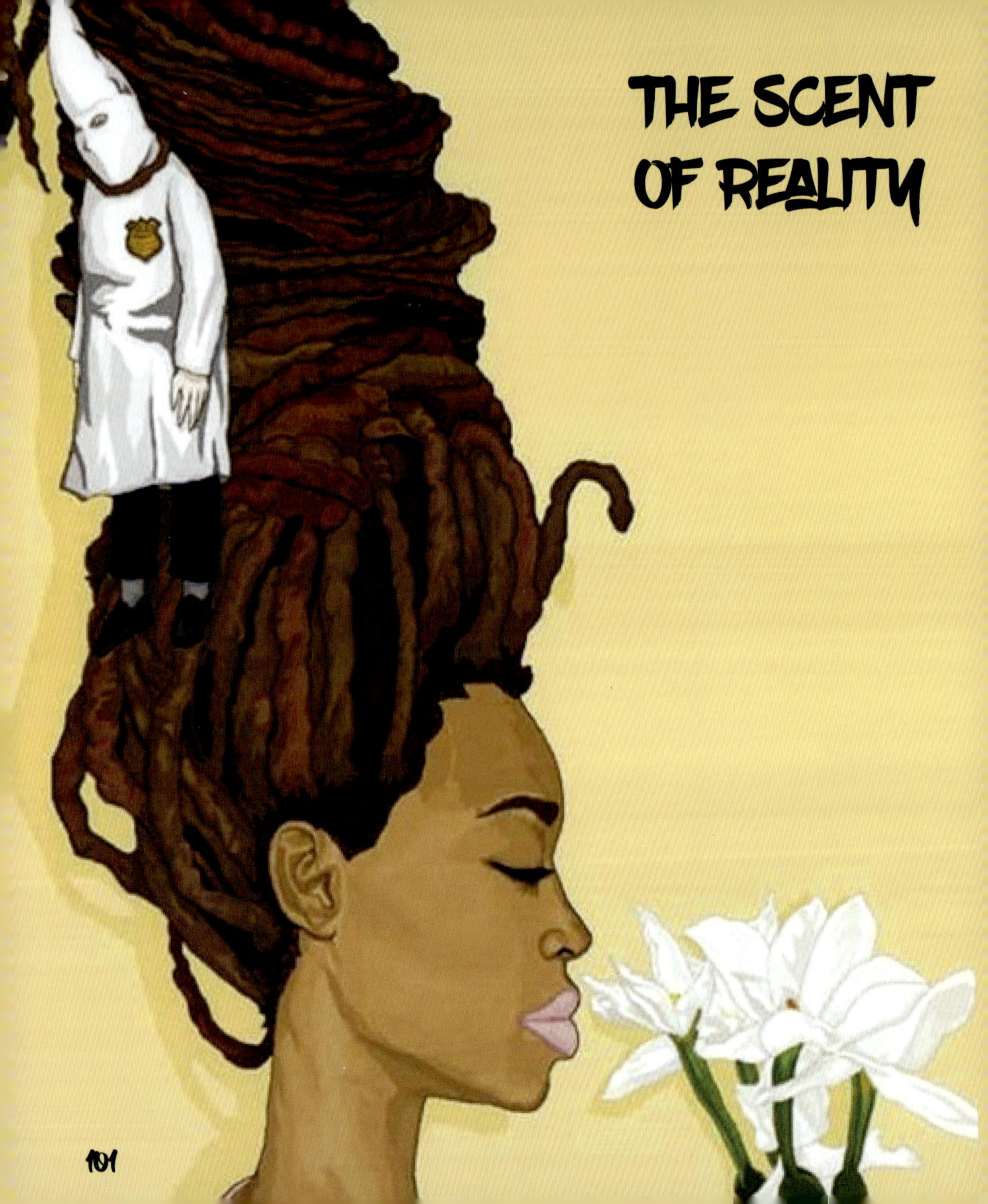

I smell the sweet flavor
of freedom from ancestors
that broke the chains
and ones who hung from trees.
The fragrance of
demolished bark,
systematic walls that block
the melanin that defines
the breath my people breathe.

The aroma of criminal element
within American society.
The self interest
capitalist hold over humanity.
The odious stench
from the ruling class
and the settlers
that deny their psychopaths.

History proves their devious acts with facts.

The sheets of the KKK
wreak
with the fear
they have
of new aged Blacks.
This melody of scents
surround notes
of peace,
prepared to wage war
against their old,
arrogant,
racist,
ways.

YOU HAD ME

You had me...

Like Mutulu
had Afeni.

Like Ossie
had Ruby Dee.

Like Nas
had Kelis.

You had me
when you shared
your poetry.

Like Elaine Brown
had Huey.

Like T.I
had Tiny

Like Lauryn
had Rohan Marley.

You had me
when you looked that officer in the eye's
and said
"every time 2 strong
black people fall in love
a klansman loses his sheet..."

You had me
when you said
"black is only a political identity."

You had me,
when your knowledge
gave my brain something to eat.

THE BLACK COLLECTION VOL. 1 : KEITH NWEZE

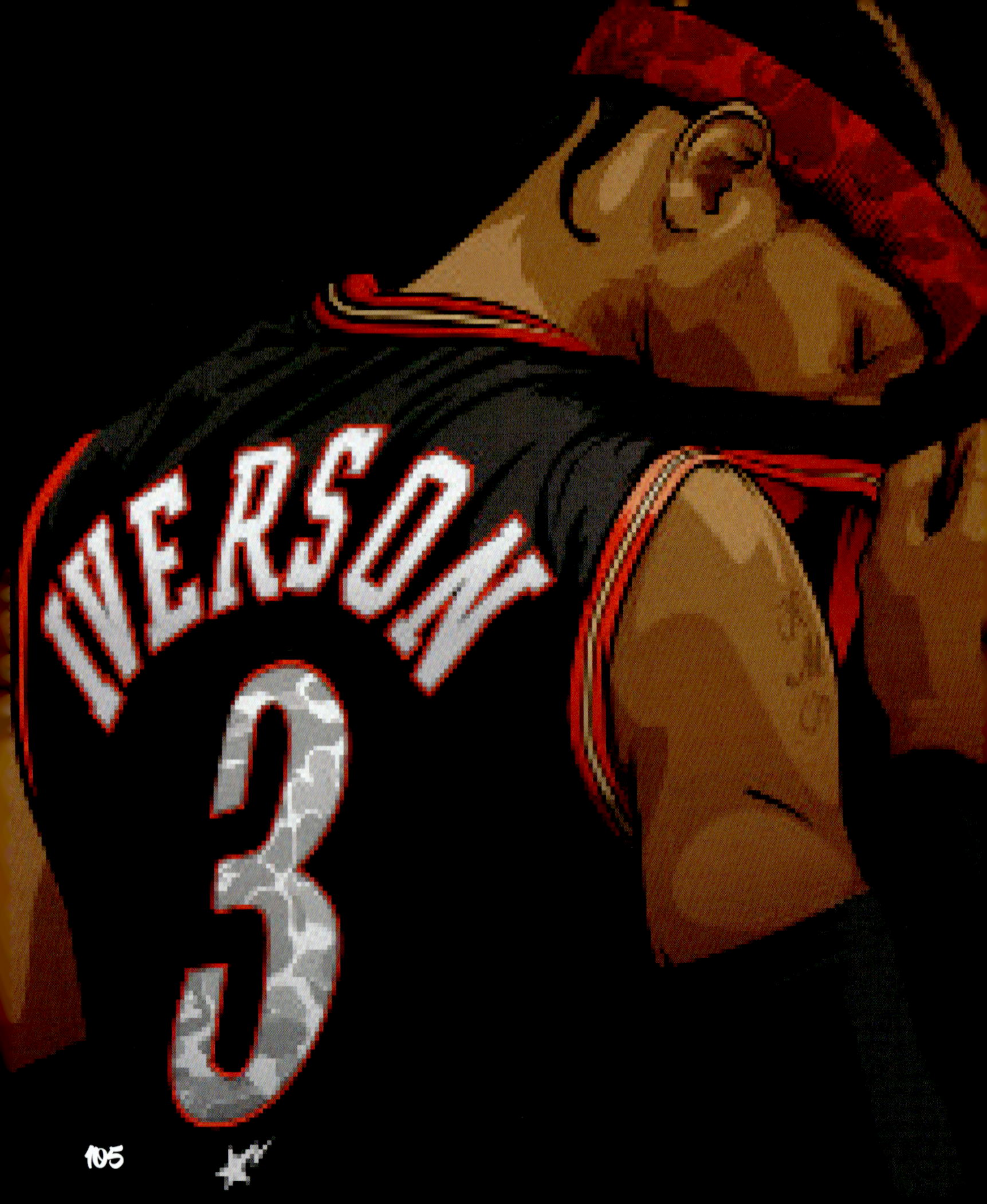
IVERSON
3

THE A.I. THEORY

Displaying heart and cultural contradictories
is the A.I. theory.

Remaining talented while living free
is the A.I. theory.

Representing an unshakeable identity with relentless pride
is the A.I. theory.

Having a rebellious mentality while willing to strive
is the A.I. theory.

Being extraordinary while representing black lives
is the A.I. theory.

Standing on two prideful feet while being misunderstood
is the A.I. theory.

Appealing to a commercial society while being an cultural icon to the hood
is the A.I. theory.

📼 Do you think Black people love America and do you think America loves Black people?

📼 What in your opinion is the best form of government for America?

📼 What does a Revolution look like?

📼 How does a group of people choose which fight is worth fighting?

THE BLACK COLLECTION VOL. 1 : KEITH NWEZE

CALL & RESPONSE
REBELLIOUS MENTALITY

109

THE BLACK COLLECTION VOL. 1 : KEITH NWEZE

111

THE BLACK COLLECTION VOL. 1 : KEITH NWEZE

SIDE B

NEWARK, WHAT HAPPENED?

Look,
if you don't believe
what I'm saying...

The apple
turned out to be a prune
or at best case
an extremely dry raisin...

The Italian community thinned,
taking the recreational opportunities
with them
as more and more
Blacks moved in.

Newark,
what HAPPENED?

THE BLACK COLLECTION VOL. 1 : KEITH NWEZE

The Irish community thinned,
taking the educational system
with them
as more and more
Blacks moved in.

Newark,
what HAPPENED?

The Jewish community thinned,
taking the banks
with them
as more and more
Blacks moved in.

Newark,
what's HAPPENING?

RILEY'S FREESTYLE

I see you Newark.
Resilient entrepreneurs
mixed with broken parents
in divorce court.

Thousands of kids searching for identity
wearing gang colors, running wild.
This freestyle
is for the child
who thinks 2 parent households
are out of style.

This freestyle
is for those working a 40-hour week
but still live in poverty.
Paramilitary agents
occupying our neighborhood,
instead of "boys in blue"
walking the beat.

I see you Newark.
Dust over townhouses
that used to be Bradley Court.

Believers
that need to be braver.
What does one do
when you're God and savior
look like your master and enslaver?

This freestyle
is for the backpack raps
with gats in it.
For the Yankee fitted
peeled back by a black menace.

Newark, we see you.
But do you see its people?

WU TANG IS FOR THE CHILDREN

WU-TANG IS FOR THE KIDS

For the moves made out of town
and the brothers and sisters lock down.
For the cold steel
around gold plated crowns.

For the bullets thrown and the tears caught
by the heartfelt.
For knowledge of self and good health.

For the chittlins and pig feet
from Mr. Charlie's leftover meat.
For the righteous free spirits unwilling to eat.

For the hope for the future
and the guilt about the past.
For the infusion of cultures
that find their way into raps.
For the 9 deep perspectives spitting on beat
where and how you live.
Wu-Tang is for the Kids!

For calling you son
because you shine like one.
For living life to the fullest
like white hot intensity of a 1000 suns.
For the ambitious entrepreneurs carrying decades
of welfare on their backs.
For the one's that asks
can it all be so simple if your born black?

For the C.R.E.A.M that sweetens our dreams.
For the true family and day 1 team.
For the thoughts and actions
that produce hood drama.
For the community in black suits
trying to comprehend the street opera.

For the one's that understand true education comes
to those willing to listen and give.
Wu-Tang is for the kids!

Hey, young world,
where are all my architects?
My creative little fingers
who used to make shit.
Build shit,
instead of putting their hands
in the next man's pocket.

Men rockin' women's clothin',
where did masculinity go?

Where did all my makeshift
cardboard dance studios go?

Where are my 2 turntables
bouncing break beats off
colorfully spray painted murals?

Where are the messages to help
the cool kids stuck in hell?

Where are the candid,
golden stories Slick Rick
used to tell?

Hip Hop is a culture
established by
poor righteous teachers
and self-educated artists.

Hey, young world,
where are all my architects?

HEY, YOUNG WORLD

121

OUR FAMILY TREE

Who will water
my family tree?
Nourish the leaves
as they grow older,
so they bloom of history.

Who will water
my family tree?
Who will strengthen
the roots wrapped around
God, culture and unity?

The devil planted fear
inside our black seeds...
50 cent sodas
got the hood going crazy.

Who will water
my family tree?
Nurture the boy and girl
that looks like you and me.

A new world
and our true destiny
resides inside your loving hands.
Just remember
it's easier to build strong children
then repairing broken men.

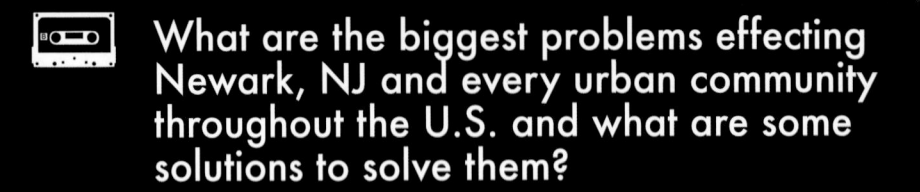

- What are the biggest problems effecting Newark, NJ and every urban community throughout the U.S. and what are some solutions to solve them?

- How important is the community to the development of your youth?

- Is there a disconnect between old and young in Hip Hop?

THE BLACK COLLECTION VOL. 1 : KEITH NWEZE

CALL & RESPONSE
THE DOWNFALL OF NEWARK

MORNING WITH YOU

Morning sex
helps me sleep
through the night.

The thought of
black lingerie covering
your chest,
has me hard by sunrise.

Your sexy voice
has us both wet.

You say
spit on it
and probe
before you
put it inside.

Be free.
Do whatever,
it's me.
Don't hide.

Finding destiny
in the motions
that gave us both life.

Hearing the screams
of instructions
to choke her harder
after each stroke.

But not too tight.

THE BLACK COLLECTION VOL. 1 : KEITH NWEZE

FOR THE MOMENT

2 lovers,
face to face.
In arms,
laying in grace.
Engulfed by a love song,
her voice is muffled.
Struggling
to seductively say,
"It's yours baby..."

Passion
echoing beneath sheets,
imprinted by lustful lips.
Breathing heavy
in anticipation of release,
embracing desire's tight grip.

Orbiting east towards fulfillment,
around distant vibrating hips.
Motions
smoother than Godiva chocolate
pulling the moment
towards ecstasy,
as she screams,
the CD skips.

"Shades of delight, cocoa hue.
Rich as the night, afro blue..."
"Shades of delight, cocoa hue.
Rich as the night, afro blue..."

Moan,
my Queen,
let it go and moan for me.
Let me taste your moans,
see your screams.

2 lovers caught in a dream,
face to face.
In arms,
beholds passion
laying in grace.

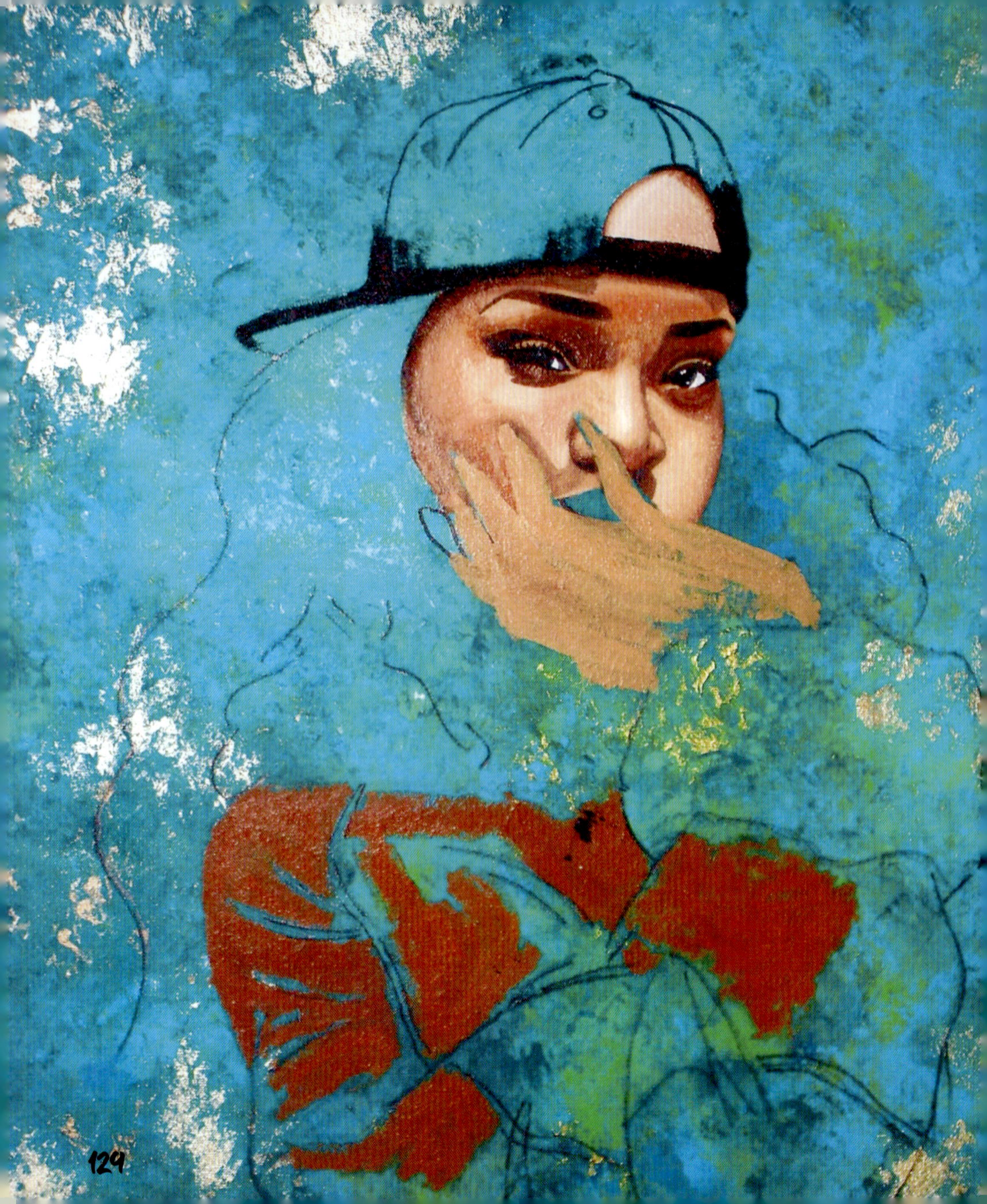

WORSHIP YOU

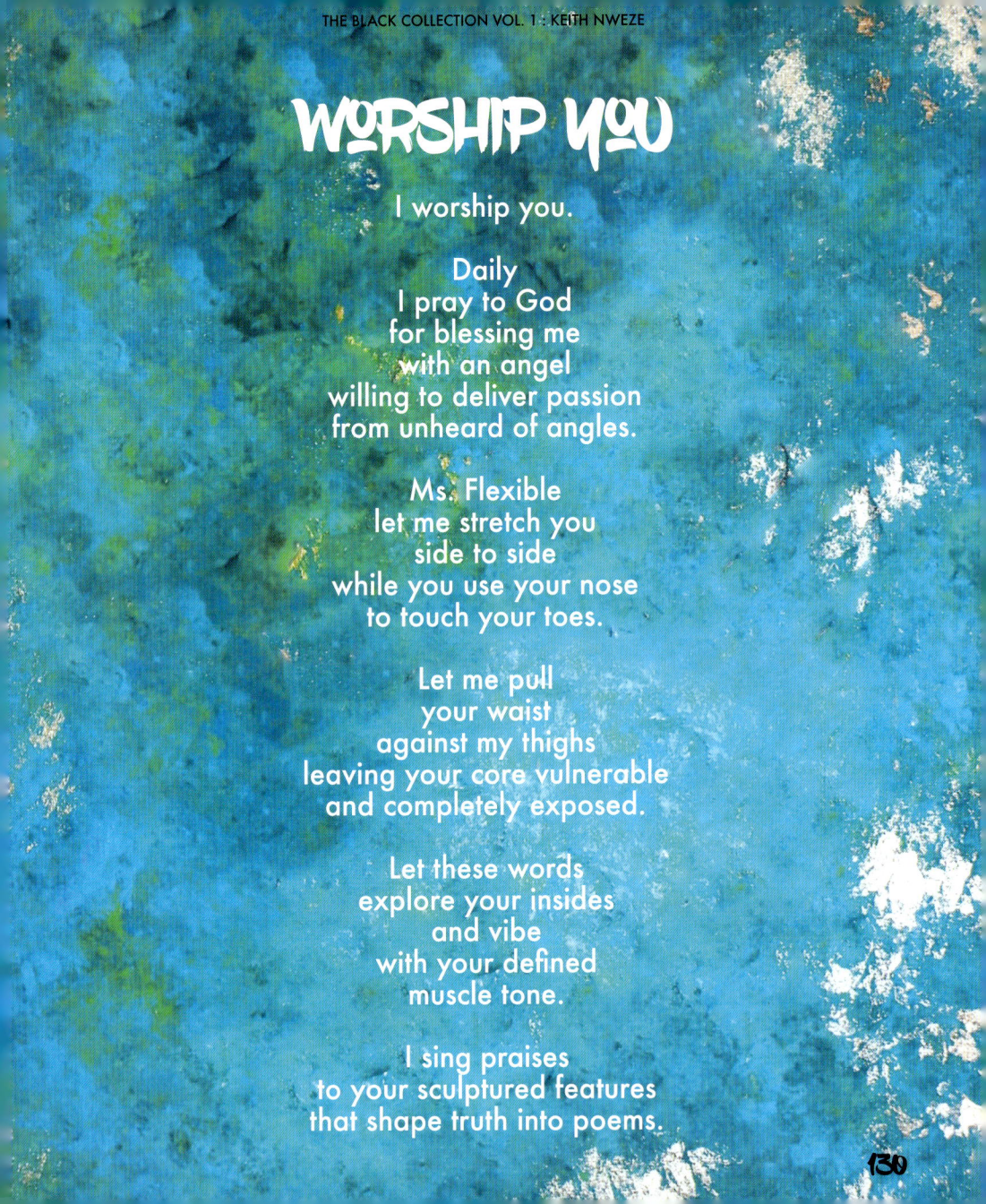

I worship you.

Daily
I pray to God
for blessing me
with an angel
willing to deliver passion
from unheard of angles.

Ms. Flexible
let me stretch you
side to side
while you use your nose
to touch your toes.

Let me pull
your waist
against my thighs
leaving your core vulnerable
and completely exposed.

Let these words
explore your insides
and vibe
with your defined
muscle tone.

I sing praises
to your sculptured features
that shape truth into poems.

131

SATURDAY WITH A QUEEN

That wifey/chill chick.
That compatible Saturday morning chill shit.
That cheese eggs, turkey bacon, and grits.
That 2 rolled, 1 lit.
That sensitive to the touch, full lips.
That thick
beautiful panty line
around voluptuous hips.

That new age ebony romantic shit.
That victorious lovemaking after watching the Knicks?!

That Porzingis!
That soft touch,
long reach
cunnilingus.

That deep, athletic dick.
That feeling of fulfillment.
That Saturday King and Queen shit.

TIME FOR YOU

I make time for you.
Grind
because you make me
feel special.

Shine because of you.

You magnetize my mind
with your lips,
massaging all pain and truth.

When I'm lonely
I think only of you.

Throbbing with anticipation,
remembering the sweet ejaculation
held by you.

Masterfully taken by you.
Satisfied because of you.

Turkey wings and head
delivered in a multicolored
Victoria's Secret bra and panty set
before picking the kids up from school.

Thankful for the time
you set aside for me
to have you.

THE BLACK COLLECTION VOL. 1 : KEITH NWEZE

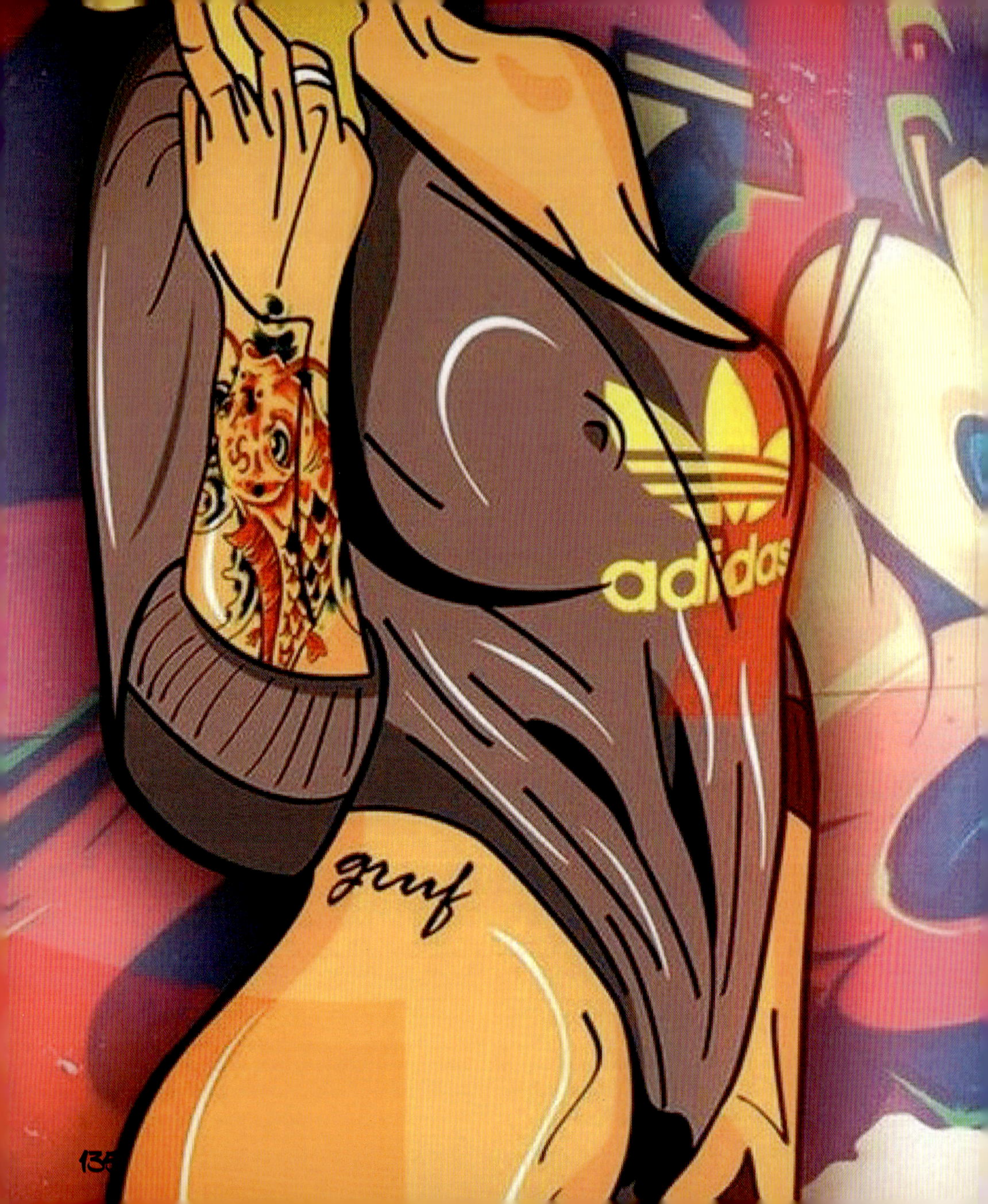
adidas
gruf

WALLS

Rhythmic
circular
strides
mix with
long
penetrating
lies.

I love you so much,
is the story moaned
as her essence
eludes my touch.

Strokes
doing
any and everything
to capture
her wet
and warm presence,
for she
is my glory
and I love the way
she makes me feel.

Completely ignoring
her back story.

How she barely
knows me,
how her screams
asked to stay
together for eternity.

Her words
evoked in me
a pity
for her
that had no name.

Still going,
completely in the moment
answering yes
even though I don't
feel the same.

My honesty
and brain
fell victim
to my lustful flaws.

Hearing emotions
that are half insane,
wondering what the heart
would say if these walls could talk.

LOVE LEAVES A THE ROOM

God,
is this more than a fuck?
Rotating love inside my Earth
dangerously caressing her thighs
as the moment flows through her hair

Pride
pulling on her Vicki straps
exciting vibes
Making love
2 a goddess
decorated in white

My obscene intervention.
I explore the depths
of her pleasure unknown
with aggressive flair

She screams
passionately
delivering life's nastiest lessons

Am I falling in love
to get hurt?
Am I growing
in her love
simply to find my worth?

Feeling fully exposed
I watch the nectar
drip from her thighs
Hoping
to clean up morals
right before church

She pieces together
loose decisions inside her purse
A union of 2
can be love
if the heart is ready
and willing to consume

But sacred parts and hearts
go their separate ways
as love leaves the room

FORGIVE ME JANET

Forgive me, Janet.
For my soul
is 1 of the million unknown statuses
roaming the planet.

Unprotected,
far from home,
lust and sins tempted me
while in Nevada.

Swaying my trust
and lust
along when she said
she's undetectable
and consistent with her Truvada.

Now my pride lays
trapped inside
a dark undiagnosed jail.

Too masculine to get tested
to check my own T-cells.

My raw decisions
have brought hell
to our loving planet.

For that I'm deeply sorry,
please forgive me,
Janet.

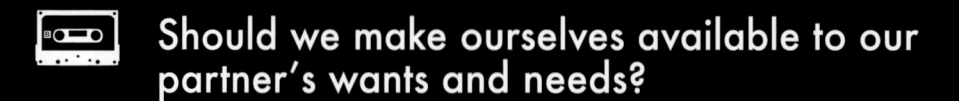

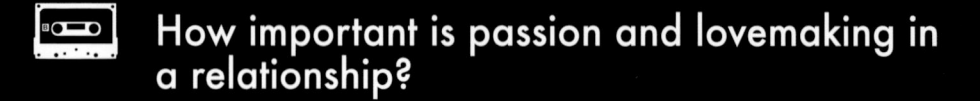

- Should we make ourselves available to our partner's wants and needs?
- How important is passion and lovemaking in a relationship?
- What does love look and feel like to you?

THE BLACK COLLECTION VOL. 1 : KEITH NWEZE

CALL & RESPONSE

RELATIONSHIPS, PASSION, & ISSUES

143

VIDEO SIRENS

When God wants you to grow,
he makes you uncomfortable.
What if that was your daughter
on TV exposed?

A Jezebel filmed to embody lust.
What if your mother was only
viewed as an object of desire,
only worthy enough to fuck?

What if the pole was the only way
to make a decent salary?
What if all the slave masters
came back
to show how exploitation
and pimping
became reality?

Would you respect us more
if you lived our history?

Or would you still love those
video hoes more than me?

145

HER POWERS

She has superpowers.

Inner strength
stronger than the logo between
her tities,
stronger than the sexual
appetite society knowingly serves
young Black Queens,
her righteousness
fiercely
and consciously devours.

She has superpowers.

Faster than lazy welfare hoes,
more powerful than the non-voting Negros,
x-ray vision spotting all the Instagram lies
the hood mentality chooses to post,
able to withstand corporate glass ceilings,
gender complaints,
baby mama feelings,
the educational system
and the ignorant local gang members
for hours.

She has superpowers.

A JERSEY THANG

Club music
is a Jersey thang.

Feet and hips
moving side to side.

Submerged in the rhythm,
lost in the vibes.

Eyes closed –
dancing with the mirror,
allowing the tempo
to direct their souls.

Embracing the high,
two-stepping
passionately
on beat
never losing control.

THE BLACK COLLECTION VOL. 1 : KEITH NWEZE

Old and young groovin'
to songs created
generations ago.

"You are my Friend"
"Superman"
"Follow Me"
"Wonderful"

Reminiscing over the
mountains of powder thrown
on Zanzibar's dance floor.

Wired by new school energy
and ecstasy
sweating bullets inside Marlo's.

Club music
is a Jersey thang.

COOKOUT WEATHER

Charcoal and burnt meat simmering.
The weather condition loudly
moves and grooves
through the summer air.
Filled bellies vibin' to old school club music,
brown sandals 2 steppin'
next to all white Nikes as kids eat
vanilla ice cream with no care.
Aunt Shirley
staring at Uncle Jerome with disgust
as he downs his
10th beer
intoxicated with lust,
sweating in heat,
Uncle Johnny surveys everythin'
with a veteran's stare.
"Damn she's a beast,"
describing the orange
Sunkist color sundress hugging
Ms. Jones' voluptuous hips.
A voice nods and disagrees,
motioning to the lime green Goddess
eating big juicy chunks of watermelon
with full strawberry
flavored lips.
Screams from the spades table turns
peace into summer madness.
Grannies' "R.I.P. Stop the Violence" t-shirt
puts the argument into perspective,
forcing suppressed tensions to reminisce.
These times spent with friends and family creating
memorable cookout moments.
Well, there's nothing more precious.

WEEKEND VISITS

Because you're a reflection
of me
and I told you to...

Girl,
don't roll your eyes
at me!
You better
go get the big pillow
and turn on Nick Jr.
while I search for your bag
of colorful barrettes.

There's a half a bag
of Nathan's thick cut fries
and 7 Gordon fish sticks left.

Don't worry
if Daddy has no food.
Just remember
what
one would do
if they truly
love you.

Yes, baby,
I love your mother as much
as I love you.

Yes,
you're special
and your mother
is a Queen,
all these things are true.

No need
to wish upon a star,
there's benefits
from loving your mother
from afar,
you have 2 sets of toys
and 2 big beautiful rooms.

Your heart
will never feel a void,
just remember
what
one would do
if they truly
love you.

Now stay still
and let daddy
do what I do.
Technically unsound,
combing the wrong way,
breaking all the rules.

Trying to execute
a tiny twist
with a Polly Pocket ponytail,
remembering the drama
I put my sister's
Barbie dolls through.

I have no idea
of what I'm doing.
Things one would do
when they truly
love you!

THANKSGIVING TIPS

Mama said
either leave the club
or find another form
of childcare.

I gave her
Uber fare and a hug
fully aware
that the people I love
don't want me there.

If they felt the groping
and the amount of money made
from deep throating,
their waning support would disappear.

If he knew I understood
the depths of his inferiority complex,
that most insecurities
are masked with sex,
he would know that I know
what lies behind his stares.

But the atmosphere and temptations
are like a drug working overtime,
catering to my addictions.

I skipped the gathering in the kitchen
to count my side hustle from the strip club
on Thanksgiving.

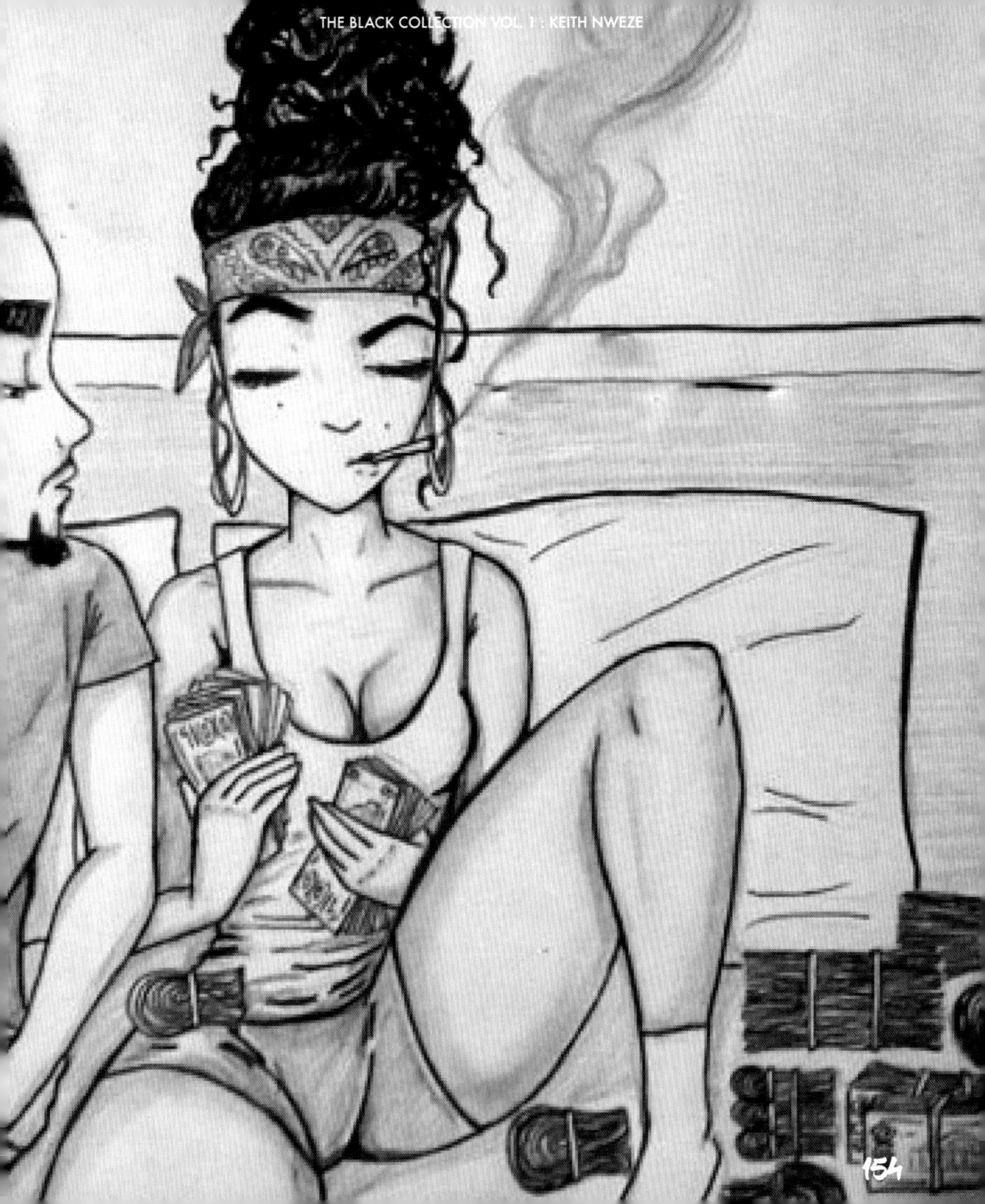

- What are your favorite cookout memories?
- What's your favorite club song?
- Is there an authentic Black experience?
- How much truth should we share with our kids and at what age?

THE BLACK COLLECTION VOL. 1 : KEITH NWEZE

CALL & RESPONSE
FAMILY AND FRIENDS

156

NEWARK BIKE FEST

THE BLACK COLLECTION VOL. 1 : KEITH NWEZE

Doom consumes us alike.
Celebrating Mother's Day by
videotaping the demise
of a young child's life.

Men search behind your eyes
asking what have we learned,
what happened to our insight?

Tires burn as joy leaves the Earth,
blood rushing out the roar of life.

Men – the community for that matter,
what are your thoughts
on another child murdered,
videotaped and ignored
at an event
that was supposed to showcase bikes?

To be deranged.
To be lonely...estranged from all living things.

Camera phones out, no one does anything.
No one helps the screams.
No one covers the scene.

Zooming in on a roaring breath losing its life.
Doom consumes us alike.

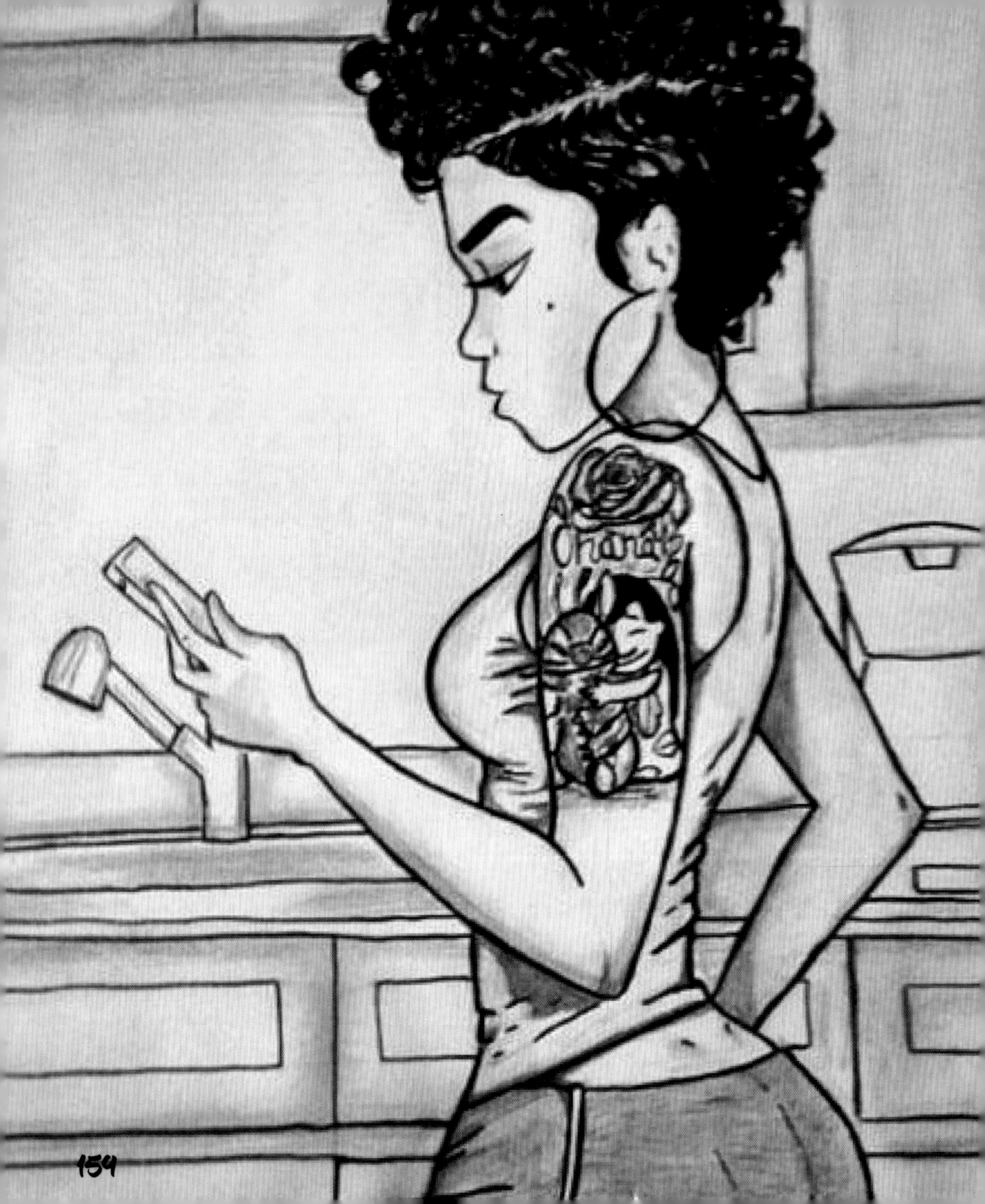

BEAUTY BECOMES UGLINESS

Her glowing character
is mixed with air feeder beauty.

Coldly staring at the blaze
on the screen as she reads
the temperature of the scene.

Hearing the shitty symphony sing
15 seconds of horror
posted on his Instagram of all things.

Watching her clone
kiss her soulmate
like a fucking saxophone.

Regretfully scheduling
a visit to the abortion clinic alone.

Bleaching his clothes
to clean the emptiness in her pits.

If the character stays
then ugliness becomes beauty?
If there is none,
does beauty become ugliness?

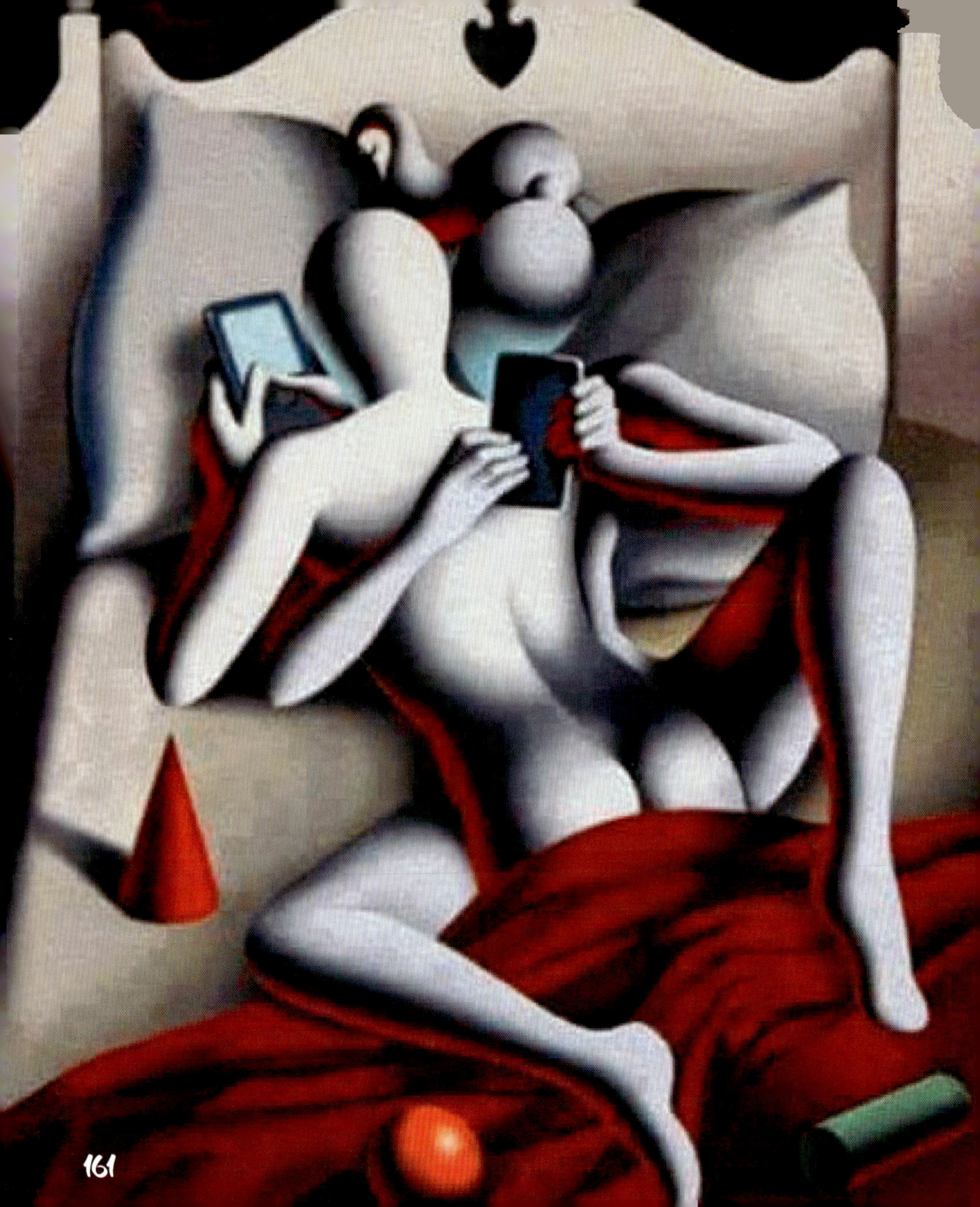

DIGITAL PEOPLE

2 people on 1 accord
are stronger than many
who disagree.

No longer
do we talk
or date
to find intimacy.

Bypassing love-making
to finesse the screen
and tap pictures of self.

On top of each other
telling Faacebook, I can
conquer myself with
your help.

Embracing virtual love
more than old school
interaction
and simple trust.

We are what our thinking
makes us.

163

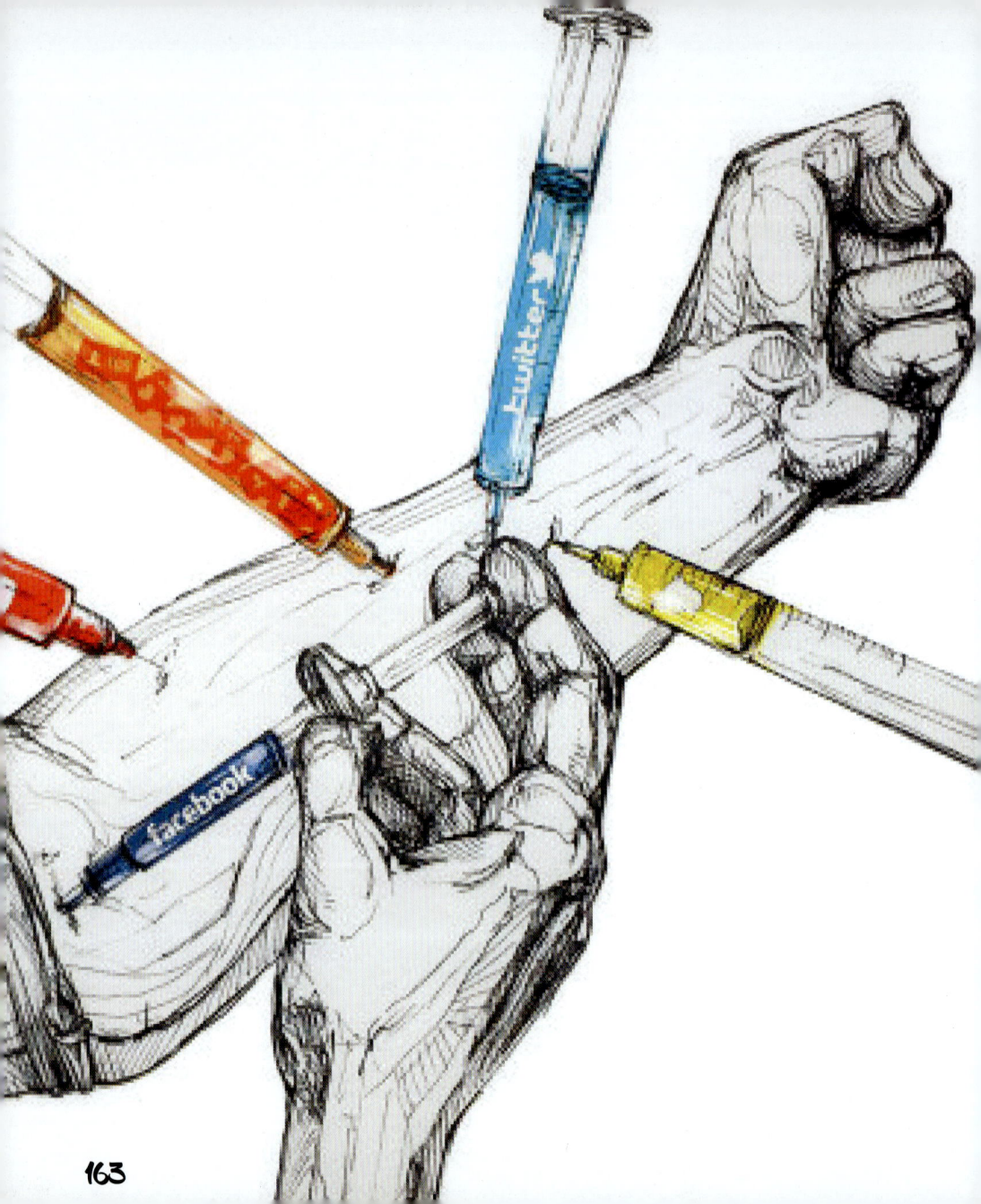

SOCIAL ADDICTION

Addicted to likes,
views,
comments
and shares.
Is this my life,
tamed by an ego
to wild to compare?

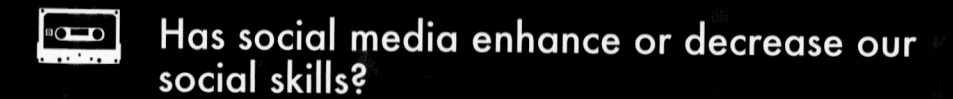

- Has social media enhance or decrease our social skills?

- Has social media desensitized us from human interaction and social tragedy?

- Are today's relationships a byproduct of Reality TV?

THE BLACK COLLECTION VOL. 1 : KEITH NWEZE

CALL & RESPONSE
SOCIAL MEDIA

166

DARK ALLIANCE

Shout out
to the scorching hot story
too true to tell.
Rest in peace Gary Web
and to the pages of "Dark Alliance"
burning in hell.

Shout out
to the devil's day
and the faithful one's
who prayed for God to stay.
Bless the poor souls that still feel
the effects of Contra,
crack cocaine
and
the untouchable
C.I.A.

THE BLACK COLLECTION VOL. 1 : KEITH NWEZE

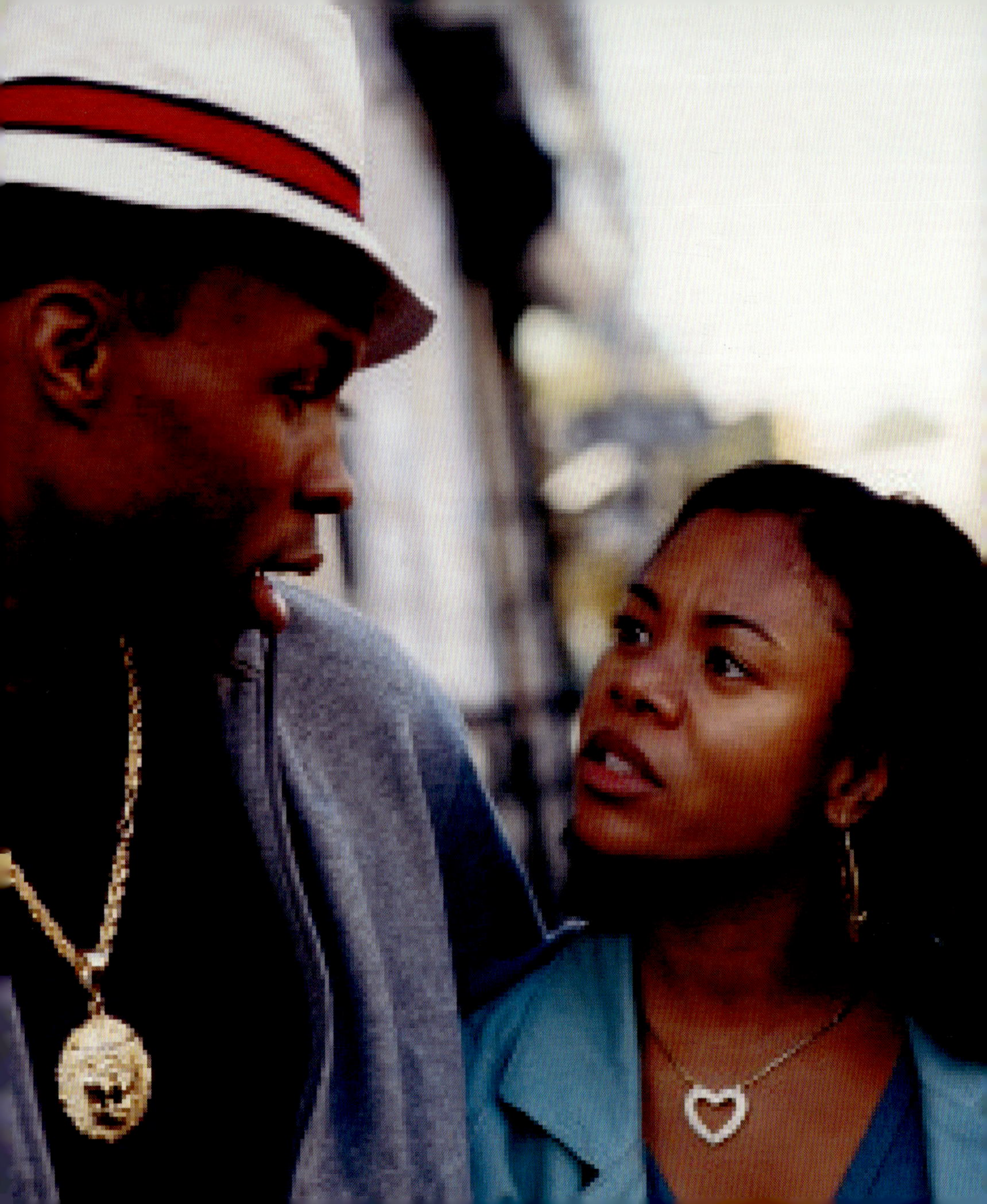

PAID IN FULL AND BORING

I love you
more than Rich loves
the game.

More than
the flashy things
that come with fame.

That's why
I tuck my chain
and leave the club
early.

People watching you
watching
me
trying to see
if their guns are worthy.

No matter
how much money
I throw out
my
drop top V
to the hood.

They only see my
success
as I race
to my highest good.

Reaganomics changed
good men into killers
like Fall weather.

Let's get money baby,
as long as
you're willing
to be boring together.

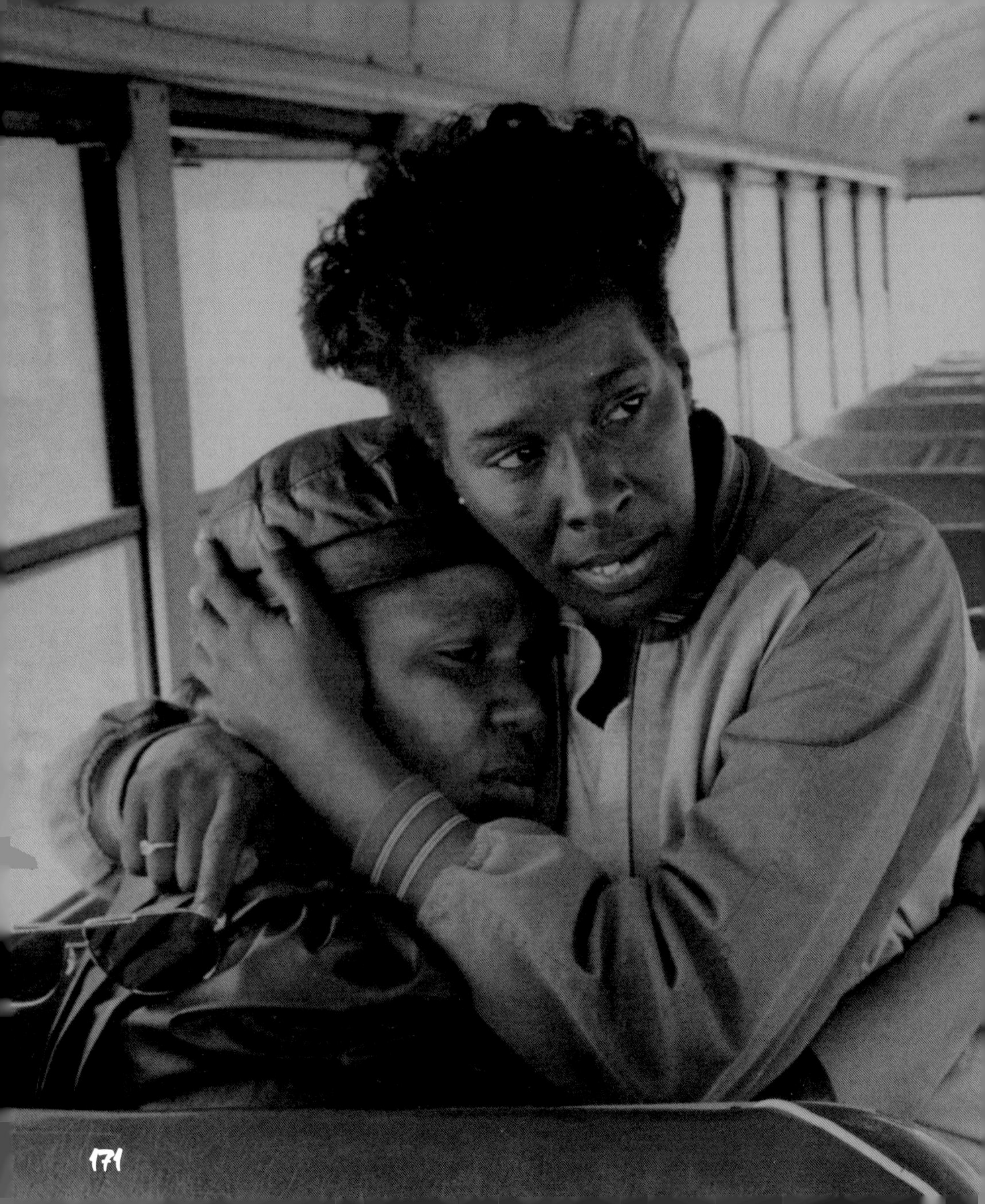

GIVE MORE

As the wind blows...
I feel
the holes in her ShopRite bag tied in knots,
trying to sell ripe sweet potatoes to feed the moment.
I see
the cocaine and snot
dripping on her malnourished lips.
I hear
the voice of desperation in need of a fix.
I understand
her logic and bullshit sales pitch.
I nurse
and support the process of lowdown Capitalists.
I give more
when I don't have it.

Now how am I going to pay the rent?

173

FEELING HER

I see the pleasures of now
and the curiosity of yesterday meeting.

I see youngin's blowing exotic haze
all the time
and the ones who only do it sometimes.

I see the old man
who smokes to keep from going blind,
eagerly opening his special delivery from
Denver
where it's not a crime.

I see the Narcos
and closet smokers puffing together.
I see the deprived wife,
high and sensitive as hell,
screaming to her husband,
"Goddamn, you feel so much better!"

I see everything
in a suffocating
slow reality,
watching the motion of her lips
inhale and drown me.

Smoking the moment
to the moment,
holding a clip
sinking in my own sea.

175

FOCUS AND LEARNING WHILE BURNING

Refocus and unlearn.
Advice given to her
grandson as she patiently
awaits her turn.

Envisioning the days
of mid-grade under the sun
as the potent haze burns.

Burning inside for not exhaling
good advice to her kids.

Married twice
so she knows what a perfect
marriage is.

Around red eyes
and red bandannas tied tight.
Her iron lungs offer evaporating advice to frail
ribs.

Coughing up smoke twice her size
because her grandson is married to the streets
with 20 other kids.

ORIGINS OF THUGGERY

And the world passed on.

Behind the eviction notice
resides the origins
of the Trap Song.
Voicing the ministry
of street energy.
The church of criminology
teaches violent chemistry.

City stories.
Gritty stories.

Like when Raheem
was voted hood mayor.
And cold glares and arguments
were settled by
shooting the fair.
And the bullets holes and broken windows
at Baxter Terrace would
sit and stare.
Like old men
fully and sadly aware.

THE BLACK COLLECTION VOL. 1 : KEITH NWEZE

Project stories.
Gang set stories.

Kill the boy,
let the man be born.
Rapping about guilt on beat,
Trying to feed the fam,
listening to
"What We Do Is Wrong."
Giving everything
to a neighborhood that doesn't
know who I am.
Labeled a thug,
forgetting God's the plug
with a plan.
Praying in my 2 hands
as you digest this image
of poverty and love
with your own 2 eyes.
An exaggerated slice
of Newark life.

179

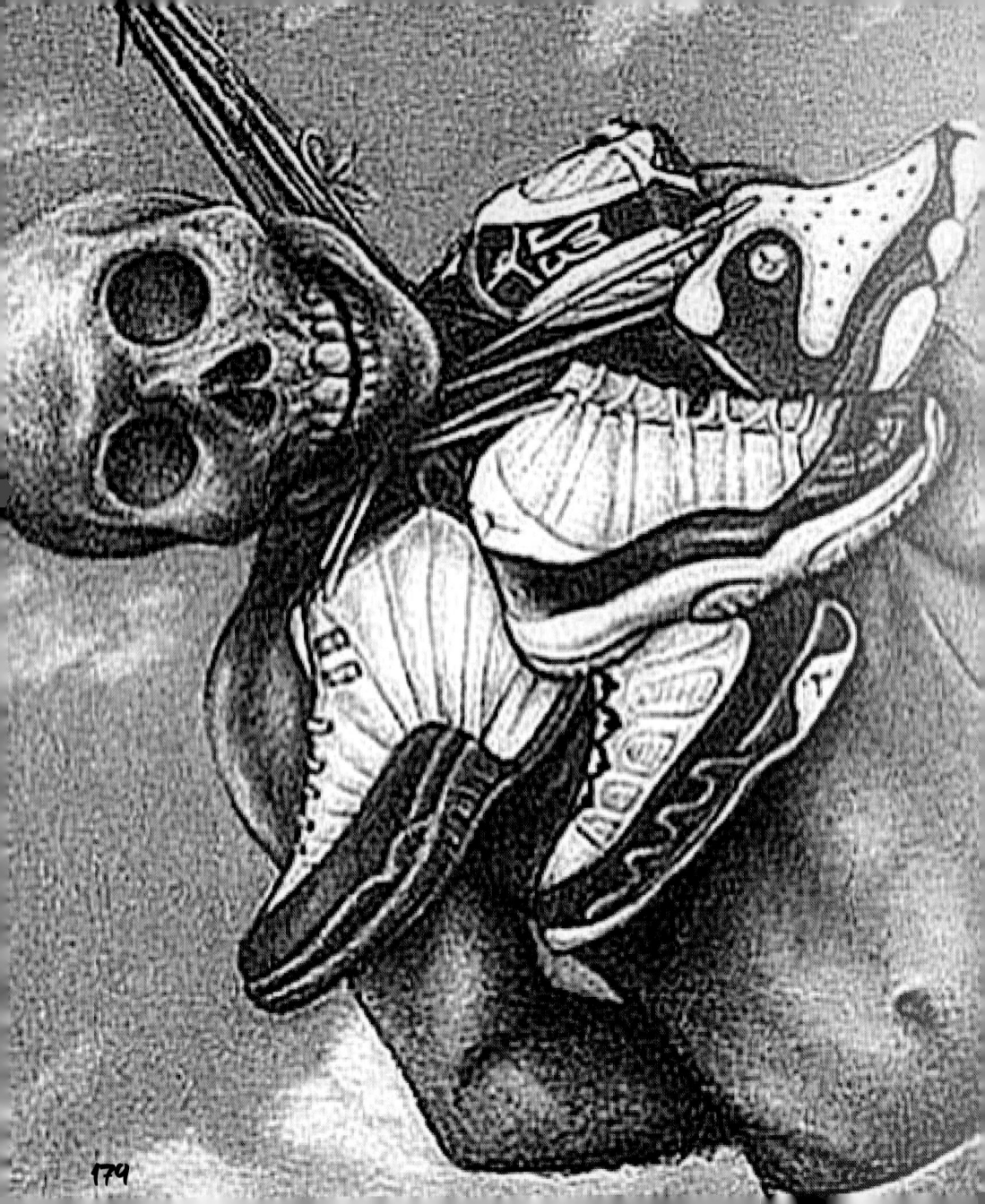

TOE TAG AIRS

Commerce over consciousness,
buried thoughts
underneath, disappear.

Can he see the funerals
soaring up there?
Would Mr. Air
give a breath
to the poor sole
without a pair?

The hole in my soul
tries to coansole
my dearly departed self-esteem,
as they roast
the fake Jordan's
on my feet.

Reading my boy's obituary
in search of retro's...

There lays a body
bought and sold for $350,
shoelaces still tied around
his throat.

His killers
are in warehouses
all around the country,
waiting for their
toe tag parole.

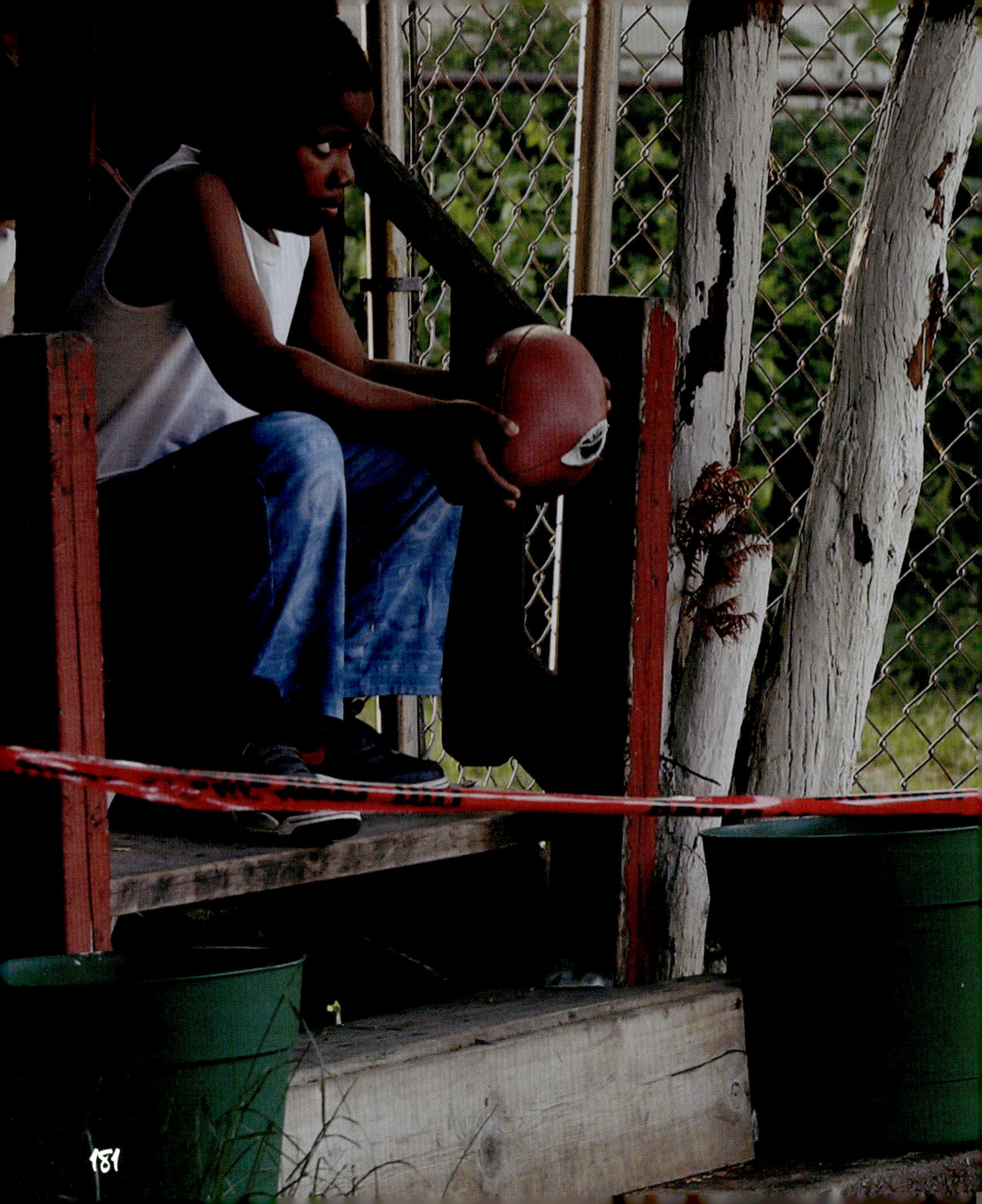

THE BLACK COLLECTION VOL. 1 : KEITH NWEZE

STOP THE VIOLENCE

Their voices
moved like Self-Destruction in the 80's.

Collectively,
their feet
marched for peace.

Marched in unison
through the veins of harmony.

Their hearts
sang for the fallen and silenced.

Their hearts
sang for Newark,
ladies and gentleman please,
"Stop the Violence!"

Emotions hit
my knees.

My throat asang
for the blood
that flowed.

Up the road,
down the road,
under the road,
above the road.

I sang
hitting all the wrong notes.

Messing up all the lyrics
with no shame.
I sang
for life
and here I quote,
"Stop the Violence!"

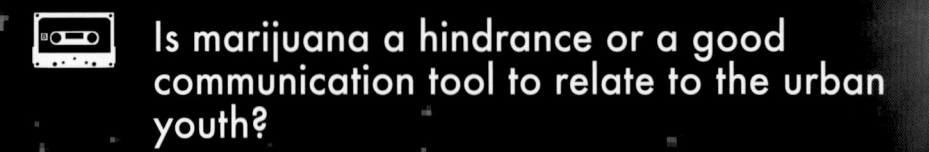

- 📼 Is marijuana a hindrance or a good communication tool to relate to the urban youth?

- 📼 Where does addiction come from and what does it look like?

- 📼 Are criminals born or created?

- 📼 Do we value material things more than Black lives?

- 📼 Do you think that a classless society, in an economic sense, is possible?

THE BLACK COLLECTION VOL. 1 : KEITH NWEZE

CALL & RESPONSE
STREET LIFE & IGNORANCE

184

HOW ARE WE?

Newark
are we a miracle defined
by tragedy?

Defined by what we see.
Defined by the word's we speak.
If words were people
'nigger'
would be a celebrity.

Shout out to the stars
of the Reconnect Program
for finding the homeless population housing.

How are we gonna win
if we ain't right within?

Newark
are we a miracle defined
by tragedy?

Defined by a lack of diversity.
Defined by the inability to read.

If buildings were people
unemployment
would be a celebrity.

Shout out to Shawn Ohazuruike
for being the first Newark
resident to win the prestigious
Princeton prize for race relations.

How are we gonna win

if we ain't right within?

Newark
are we a miracle defined
by tragedy?

Defined by what we believe.
Defined by what we achieve.

If drugs were people
crack
would be a celebrity.

But with education,
hard work and opportunity
things evolve into other things.

Shout out to 110 Williams street
and all the workers
down to fight
and prevent poverty.

A shining example
of black excellence,
opulence
and decadence.

How are we gonna win
if we ain't right within?

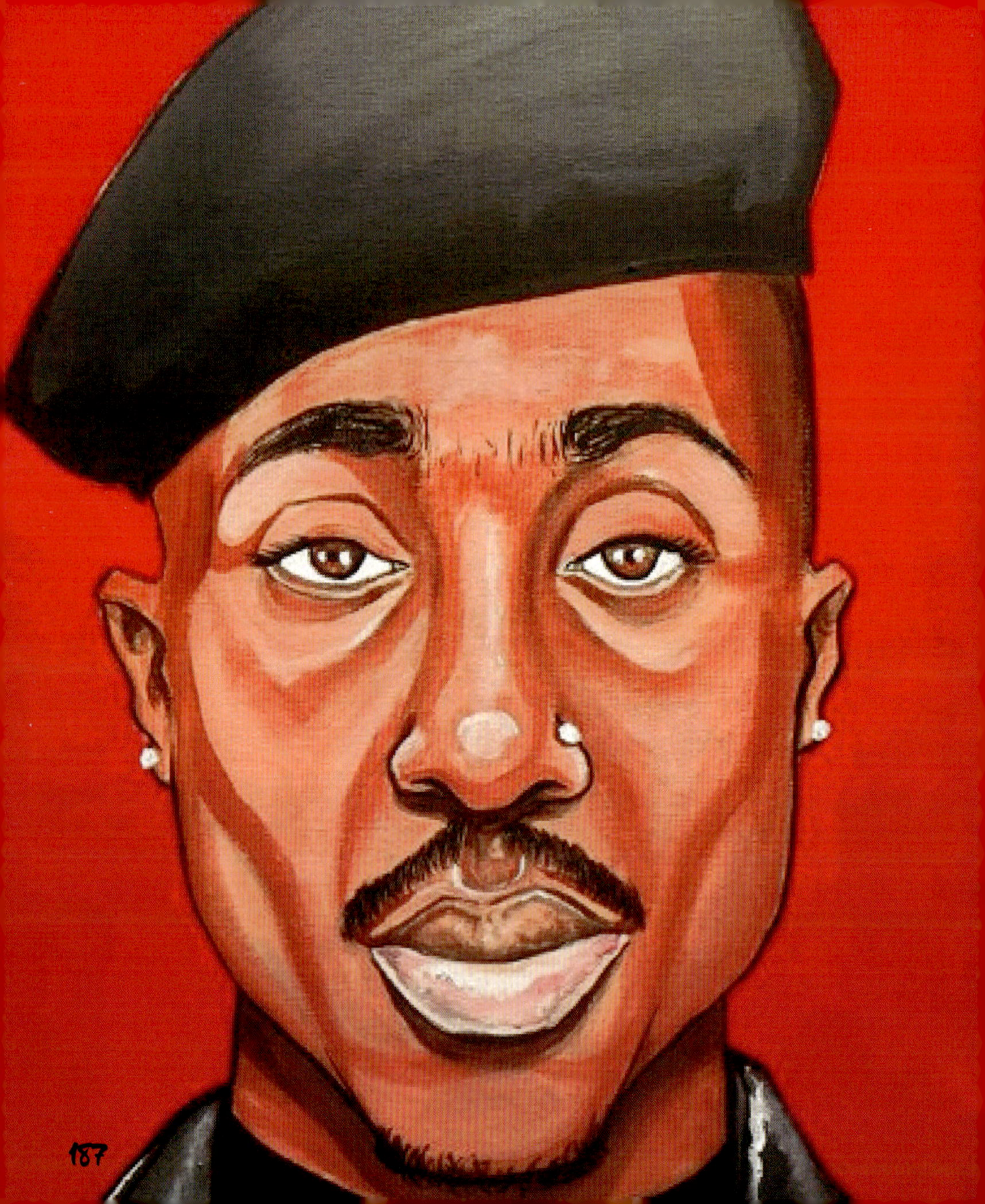
187

RISE... IF YOU'RE READY FOR CHANGE

Rise...
RISE!

Wake up
my morning glories.

Wake up
my beautiful black seeds.

Taste the green fruit
of materialistic rebellion.

Feed yourself the truth,
my prisoners of starvation.

Rise,
you wretched
of the Earth.

Let your voice rise
so we can hear
the joyous cries
of a better world in birth.

GET IN FORMATION

Black fists get in formation.
Form a unified line
ready to build a black nation.

Africa for Africans.
Here or there we must
embody the Motherland within.

Like Marcus Garvey
or the Talented Tenth.

Travel through the growth
and destruction of the Black man.

Like Kwame Ture
or Fred Hampton.

The knowledge to win
resides here
not in the hereafter.

As long as we're willing to care
and convince ourselves
Black lives really matter.

Black like believing in
the spectrum of blind faith
and better days.

Black like the breakfast programs
established to help the community
find its way.

Black like how we made
savages into nigger,
coon into boy,
negro into the President
America now has today.

Black fists all over the globe
get in formation.

Unified hands,
let's build our homes
into a beautiful
black nation.

Be... For Newark

Be...
the brain that holds Common Sense
Be...
the evolution of Malcolm X
Be...
the message from the heart
Be...
the thought willing to do its part
Be...
above State controlled education
Be...
the resident that stops gentrification
Be...
the direction of Ras Baraka
Be...
the health care from Obama
Be...
the hand that feeds the homeless
Be...
the prick administrating an HIV test
Be...
the reason why someone is blessed
Be...
the love during sex
Be...
the hug to support the mess
Be...
the thug unwilling to settle for less
Be...
the peace invading Newark life
Be...
in the streets
for the city,
down and ready
to occupy!

THE BLACK COLLECTION VOL. 1 : KEITH NWEZE

📼 Who are you?

📼 If given the opportunity, would you be willing to rise or help someone else rise?

📼 Who are we?

📼 If 40 million Black fists united and were awarded Military Power, Economic resources and Land what would a Black Nation look like?

📼 How important is it to rally and occupy?

THE BLACK COLLECTION VOL. 1 : KEITH NWEZE

CALL
& RESPONSE

RHYME BOOK

100 sheets • 200 pages

ACKNOWLEDGEMENTS

All praises to the Most High.
I know and believe you're the generator behind these poems and messages. I'm deeply humbled by the gift you've bestowed upon me.

Peace and love to my mother, Geoff, Eric, Kyree, Laila, Queen Essence and Iman. Without your direct contact and support I wouldn't be able to function and reach my full potential. Tai, I will never forget your encouragement and motivational nature that guided me through a dark time in my life. You have permanent residence in my heart.

Much love and appreciation to my talented and inspirational creative family. ShaVaughn Morris, Shaquanda Stephenson, Cenceara Allen, Alnisa Lucas, Rah Digga, Eric B, Muhaymin Bentley, Jah Jah Shakur, Baruti Libre Kafele, Kym Gilchrist, Elijah Muhammad, Tehsuan Glover and Todd Hoffman.

Eternal love and respect to my first History, English and Sociology teachers, Tupac, Nas, Eric B. and Rakim, Kool G Rap, Kid n' Play, Common, Ice Cube, Raekwon, Lauryn Hill, Redman, Scarface, Rick Ross, Kendrick Lamar, J. Cole, A Tribe Called Quest, Outkast, Mobb Deep, The Lox, and to every MC that spits knowledge, wisdom and love for black people and the black community.

KEITH NWEZE

AUTHOR ENTREPRENEUER

Author and entrepreneur Keith Nweze is a Houston, Texas native born to Cecile Elliot and Ike Nweze. At a young age, Keith and his family relocated to the borderline of Maplewood and Irvington, NJ where he later became a basketball varsity letter at Columbia High School and again for the Gothic Nights at New Jersey City University.

His interest in sociology and passion for helping people earned him key positions at agencies such as the Department of Youth and Family Services, Pre-College Upward Bound Program, The Hyacinth Foundation and currently, The Department of Health and Community Wellness in Newark, NJ.

Keith's community based work in the social services sector and his love for hip-hop music helped shape his passion for poetry. He finds it fascinating that thought provoking dialogue can spark from seven lines of text. Out of that same passion his company, Raw Thoughtz, LLC, was birthed. Raw Thoughtz became the platform Nweze used to self-publish six poetic masterpieces including his latest works, Struggle and The Black Collection.

Mr. Nweze's journey from growing up with a short attention span to entrepreneurship has taught him three valuable lessons: learn to grow from constructive feedback, believe in yourself no matter what and push to continually grow in your craft.

The outgoing and creative father of two (Kyree and Laila) is on a mission not likely to die down any time soon. Keith Nweze is applying his lessons learned in order to take Raw Thoughtz, LLC and his written works of art from colleges to coffee tables around the world to make reading fun in our community again.

INDEX

Reese Royce - 90, 153, 155

Van Arno - 99, 100

Jamel Shabazz - 13, 14, 109, 110

Helen Stuimmer - 84, 128, 129, 171, 177

Dale Edwin Murray - 85, 86

Denny Owusu - 52, 56

Lisete Alcalde - 35, 36

Dan Lish - 53, 54

Kuf Knotz 15, 16

Sarah Weaver 27, 28

Ashley Straker - 45, 46

Quinn McGowan - 71

EJ Brown - 80

Gabe Tiberino - 87, 88

INDEX

Mata Ruda (Karl Miller Espinosa) - 96

Leo Mancini Hresko - 97

Van Arno - 99, 100

Watson Mere - 101

Keturah Ariel 104

Bape - 106

Kevin A Williams - 126

Gruf - 135

Payle - 137

McFreshCreates - 143, 173

Mark Kostabi - 161

AcidPaint - 163, 164

James Dietz - 167, 168

Aaron Maybin - 187

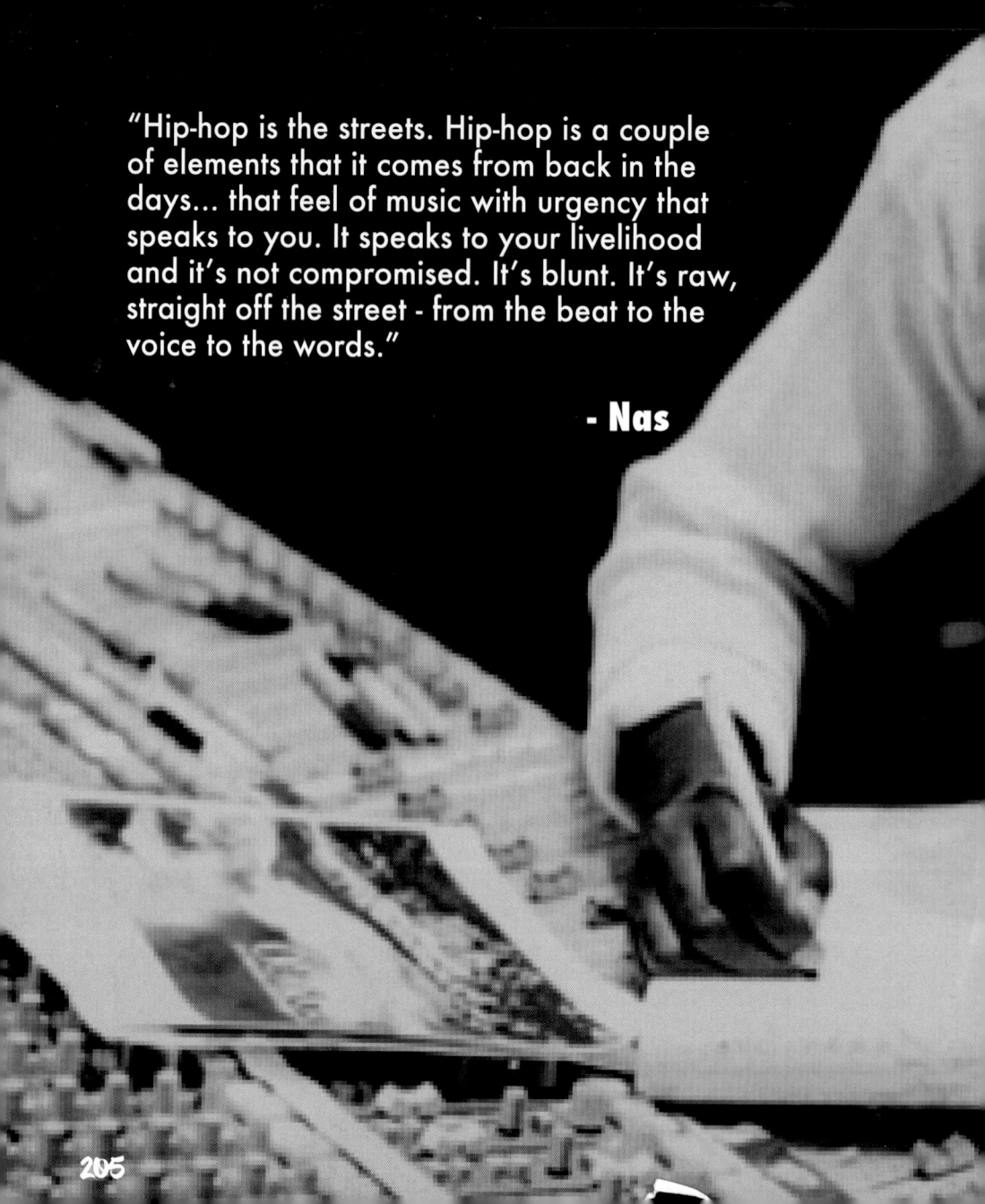

"Hip-hop is the streets. Hip-hop is a couple of elements that it comes from back in the days... that feel of music with urgency that speaks to you. It speaks to your livelihood and it's not compromised. It's blunt. It's raw, straight off the street - from the beat to the voice to the words."

- **Nas**